More
Mischievous in Mendham

a

Collection of Childhood Memories

≈

by

Gregory L. Smith

MORE MISCHIEVOUS

IN

MENDHAM

Published by Bookbaby

7905 N Crescent Blvd.

Pennsauken Township, NJ, 08110

Publication Date: November 2019

First Edition

Cover photograph: Hilltop School, Mendham, N.J. image © 2019 Gregory L. Smith

Back cover photograph: Mountain Valley Pond, Mendham, N.J. image © 2019 Gregory L. Smith

Courtesy *Morristown Daily Record*

for

Walter, my brother

— Forward —

The Village of Mendham, NJ

I have been asked what Mendham was like back in the late forties through the fifties. I feel very fortunate to have grown up in this country community and to be able to share so many good stories about growing up here in both of my books during that time period. This description of Mendham will be written from my point of view, through my eyes, as a young boy around ten years old in 1952.

Mendham was more like a small village back then, certainly not built up as it is today, with new housing developments, condominiums, and a mall. Motor vehicle traffic was light most days, increasing in volume during commuting hours. To start my tour, I've hopped on my JC Higgens™ bicycle with the big balloon tires heading down East Main Street, now 1-24E, to Joe's Tavern, about where the Exxon™ Gas station is located today. Of course, I can't go into it, but it is a good place to start my tour of Mendham, on the edge of town. I've turned around on the paved two-lane road heading back in a westerly direction, towards the center of town. Neither the Mendham Kings™ Mall nor the Ford™ dealership exists yet. However, it's where Applebee's Horse Stable is located. This is the place I used to trap fur animals until I got chased up a tree by a pack of wild horses, causing me to be late for school and sent to principal Latterlee's office.

Several hundred feet up on my right is Conroy's hamburger stand. There's an aroma of hamburgers cooking on their grill for customers standing in line at the outside service counter. There are no Burger King's™ or McDonald's™ fast food

4

establishments but, there are wonderful places like Conroy's stand and local diners to get great tasting hotdogs, hamburgers, and French fried potatoes. I can smell another wonderful aroma coming from up the road, this time sweet chocolate from Country House Candy, owned by the Price family. They produce quality chocolate candies. Often, when I palled around with their son, Billy, it was torture to play outside with the smell of chocolate floating in the air around his home wafting under my nose—much like visiting Hershey, Pennsylvania today. Unfortunately, each candy got boxed, not one went in our mouths.

Across the street from the Price's home is Rowe's Farm. It appears much as it does today, with red barns and a pasture filled with sheep grazing on the abundant grass.

Next to the Price family's home, is the New Jersey Bell Telephone™ building. Bell Tel™ is what everyone calls the company. They use operators to connect our telephone calls through a switchboard. About three hundred feet up the road is Hillcrest Road. It's the route my parents take to reach our home on Hillcrest Place.

The large home on the corner of Hillcrest and Main belongs to the Moeri family. On Sunday afternoons, the family hosts an open house for neighbors, friends, and anyone else in the town to enjoy coffee, tea, donuts, and lots of good conversation. On Sundays in the fifties, it's a state law that all stores be closed, and that includes those in Mendham. One exception is Robinson's Drug Store—you can buy prescription drugs, but nothing else, not even a scoop of ice cream. Sunday is a day of rest, to attend church, or visit family.

On the corner of Orchard and Main is Dr. Hopper's medical practice. His patients are expectant Mendham area mothers and somehow, me. One of my childhood curiosities is, why do I sit in this doctor's waiting room with a bunch of women with fat bellies, when I'm a young boy, skinny as a rail?

Across the street from the doctor's office is a home with a pond and brook behind it.

Mendham kids like to explore this brook on a regular basis to look for frogs, small fish, crayfish, and snakes. It also flows past the elementary school on Hilltop Road. We explore it on our lunch breaks, sometimes arriving late for our next class.

Gunther Motors, the Chevrolet™ Dealership, is on the opposite corner on Orchard St., the only new car dealer in town. Directly across the street from them, is the Sinclair™ gas station that does automotive repairs and sells old cars. There're two Model A Fords™ out front with for-sale signs—$200! That's where Howie works when he doesn't drive the school bus to and from Morristown High School.

Next to Gunther's, is our volunteer fire department, where the town's fire engines are garaged. Many children have their very first ride on a fire engine here. What a thrill it is for me and other kids to sit high on top of the bright red, American LaFrance™ Fire Engine each year, with the siren blasting away, riding through town. In addition, on Halloween, we dunk for apples in a large tub filled with water. They're all drenched in some other kid's slobber. We don't care, as we try to bite into one. I enjoy all the fun activities up on the second floor every year I go there. It's always packed with kids having a good time.

The sidewalk on this side of the street changes from poured cement sections to huge dark gray slates, as smooth as glass. An interesting challenge to walk on without falling when rain freezes instantly on the cold slate on a winter's day—I landed on my butt many times!

The stained brown Methodist Church and the manse are a short distance up East Main Street. The white Episcopal Church is across the street.

Up the sidewalk incline, in the center of town is Mendham's first dentist, Dr. Barnett, who opened his practice recently. It's the place for Mendham kids to have their first tooth pulled or filled. We don't have preventive dentistry now. We only go to the dentist when a tooth gets bad and we can no longer stand the pain.

6

With all the sugary drinks, cookies, cakes, pastries, and candy bars we consume, he has a busy practice. We all have cavities, I have a handful and go to Dr. Barnett to have them filled.

On the corner of Mountain Avenue and Main is Robinson's Drug Store. That's where my parents buy our medications and aspirin. They not only sell medicines, gifts, and vacuum tubes, but you can sit on one of their red cushioned, art deco stools, and enjoy a delicious soda, ice cream, or my favorite, a root beer float.

Mountain Avenue is the road my elementary classmates and I have to run down to get to the town's athletic field to play baseball for gym. Further down the hill is Mendham's swimming facility, Mountain Valley Pool.

Near the pool, I can still see the remains of railroad tracks. At one time, the Rock-A-Bye Baby Train crossed Mountain Avenue. The train line ceased operation in 1913.

The historic Black Horse Inn is on the opposite corner of Mountain Avenue. Lots of families go there for a great dining experience, especially on holidays. I enjoy eating the ribs of beef entrée there. Down the road from the inn, is Laddy Freeman's service station.

Close-by Laddy's is my favorite place to visit and buy stuff, Jimmy's. This is where I buy all my balsa wood airplane kits, model ships kits, and even a .049 gas engine for my prized model airplane. It's also the place where I pretend to be a slick cowboy. When I need to buy more ammo for my B-B rifle, I come here. Jimmy may be the inventor of the password before it will be used on computers in the future.

As a kid, I have to use secret words to buy ammo. First, I have to make sure no one is around. If okay, I will go up to the store's counter and whisper to Jimmy, "I need to buy some curtain weights." Curtain weights are his two-word password to buy B-B's. Most young boys, like me, have a BB gun and need to buy them frequently.

Across the street from Jimmy's is a general store where Mendham families buy food items. One time, Mrs. Larson, my friend's mom, bought a large box of chocolate bars there for us as a snack. When we opened the brown paper candy wrappers, the almond bars were filled with tiny wiggly worms—that killed my appetite for chocolate bars for a long while.

St. Joseph's Roman Catholic Church is near the general store. I mistakenly went to this church one Friday afternoon from my elementary school, along with my Catholic classmates, when they started religious instruction—I'm Presbyterian. I was promptly escorted back to the Hilltop elementary school. I was Catholic for one day!

Returning towards the center of town, on the opposite side of the street, is the historic Phoenix House where Mendham's Police Department is located. That's where Chief Brill has his office. Lacking a jail cell, he uses an old church pew and post, complete with handcuffs. The cuffing post is used mostly to temporarily secure someone until they are either released or transferred to the Morris County Jail in Morristown. My brother, Walter Smith, is a police officer in town working for Chief Brill. The Phoenix House is where the municipal court and town hall are. The Civil Defense Group meets in the basement to practice emergency radio communications in the event of a nuclear attack. Also, Hilltop Presbyterian Church uses the Phoenix house on Sunday mornings for my Sunday school class.

On the opposite corner is a private butcher, Moeri's Meat Market. Here, you can buy quality meats. However, most families, including mine, travel to Morristown to shop at the A & P™ or at another supermarket, where meats and groceries cost less than in town.

Near Moeri's is Keupferle's hardware store. They have all the items for building and repairing household projects. I'm a regular customer, buying parts to build crystal radios. Cub and Boy Scouts come here to buy antenna wire, enameled covered wire to wind coils, Galena crystals, and cat's whiskers to build their simple crystal radio project to obtain their merit badge.

Another favorite place of mine, a few steps away, is Joe's Luncheonette. They have counter food, coffee, and all sorts of smokes. Most people are addicted to smoking cigars, pipes or cigarettes, sometimes all three. There are only a few places where you can't have something on fire dangling from your mouth: church, school, and the doctor's examination room. Joe's is the place where all the kids and I buy our candy and gum. Chewing gum is popular, not only for the thin pink slab of gum inside the wrapper, but for the picture of a famous baseball player next to it. We treasure these cards! We can't wait to rip off the paper to see what baseball player is inside. Often, we trade them to have a complete collection of players. There are lots of magazines and comic books, along with several newspapers here, too. My favorites are *Popular Mechanics* and *Popular Electronics*. Unfortunately, I don't have enough change in my pocket to buy one. So, when no one is looking, I just pick them up, thumb through them, and drool over all the stuff to build before returning them to the rack.

Hilltop Road at the center of town is where the Pastime Club is. If you are a member, you can bowl here. Close by is the town's barbershop. Across the street are the United States Post Office, public library, and elementary public school—K-8th grade. Further up the road, is the historic Hilltop Presbyterian Church that my family and I go to.

This concludes my little bike tour of Mendham, as I remember. I hope this will bring back many treasured memories if you lived here back in the forties and fifties.

Gregory L. Smith

Contents

Chapter 1

Elementary School:

Graham Crackers™ to Algebra

Mendham Borough, NJ 1947-56

My early education started in kindergarten at Mendham Borough Elementary School on Hilltop Road, that encompassed K through eighth grade. They had two, half-day sessions to cover student enrollment. In my classroom, each of us was assigned a cubby to store our stuff, mostly clothing items and crayons. Our class didn't start out at the educational level that children do today. Most of my classmates and I didn't know the alphabet or how to count; but, somehow knew two letters placed together 'N and O,' very well. We didn't have pre-school back then, to start us out, learning the basics; the alphabet letters, letter sounds, and numbers. I had spent my first five years of life on this earth having fun—playing. So when I arrived for my first day of kindergarten I knew very little, except, how to play, take naps, and enjoy Grahams™ and milk.

Class behavior was high on the list of priorities that my teacher had to accomplish with my class; along with listening and following her instructions and learning to interact with other children. Going down for a nap after our wonderful snack of milk and graham crackers, was no problem at all for any of us. After our teacher tamed our behavior, she had to teach us the different shapes and colors. Her challenge was to get us to memorize the *Pledge of Allegiance*. The one we learned was an earlier revision, leaving out the words, "under God." After teaching us the pledge, breaking it up, line by line, some of the kids were still getting it wrong. Tommy was having one heck of a time getting it right when he recited:

11

"I pledge alliance to the flag of the United States of America and to the public for which it stands, one nation, divisible, with liberty and justice for all."

Once a week, we had music appreciation. Our teacher would get the record player out of the AV storage area and bring it to the classroom. She would select a record, a 78, (78 revolutions per minute) and place it on the record player. We had to sit on our mats and listen to the Nutcracker's, *Dance of the Sugar Plum Fairies* and parts of Beethoven's *9th Symphony*.

When I got promoted to first grade, my classmates and I had Mrs. Garabrant as our teacher. We couldn't have gotten a better teacher. She cared about us dearly, had a nice way of correcting us without hurting our feelings and even gave us a hug when we were feeling down.

We were expecting another year of some play activity, much like we enjoyed in kindergarten. We were disappointed when we had to turn our brains on and learn how to print letters and numbers. The technology to do that was simple back then, a lined blackboard and white chalk. Some of us had a real problem with opposite formed lower case letters, d's and b's along with p's and q's. For whatever reason, my brain wouldn't work discerning d's from b's and vice versa. Of course, that went on my report card and my mother had to hire a tutor to hammer which was which into my head.

From all the hard work we did in first grade, they had to give us a break. They called it recess. The girls in my class headed for the swings and seesaws behind the school. The guys liked to play something rougher, cowboys, bank robbers, and Indians. Most recess breaks, I turned into the Lone Ranger riding my horse Silver. We played on both sides of the school that had ten-foot hedges that reached to the sky. They probably started out one time as neat, trimmed ones, but were neglected and got out of control. The hedges were a great place for bandits to hide to rob a passing stagecoach. Our imaginations were great back then.

I believe our teacher graded us on our classwork papers and her observations when we started school. We didn't have tests in first grade, those came in later grades. We got to choose our seats for the year, starting in first grade. I sat in the back with the other boys. The teacher's pets—no boys—later known as brownnosers, sat around his large wooden desk. The others sat in the middle section. Yearly school plays began in first grade, requiring us to memorize parts. Our mothers that were good with a needle and thread made the costumes at home. Most of the time, these things worked like magic in getting us into character for some silly play.

Once a week, we had an art teacher that popped into our classroom throughout the lower grades. She taught us how to draw and paint. Her arrival on a Friday, gave our teacher a much-needed break, especially after spending a week teaching us the required curriculum. I was good at drawing cars, ships, and radios, but lacked the talent to draw curves to create the human form and animals. I had to draw those with straight-line segments. When Halloween neared, my classmates and I enjoyed making orange and black glued paper rings. You could hear a pin drop in our classroom. My classmates and I worked like Ford Motor™ factory workers, gluing alternate orange and black paper rings. By the time the big clock struck, the class session was over, we had a string of rings long enough to circle the entire classroom.

In second-grade, we had Miss Ferguson, one of our stricter teachers. She taught us the building blocks of math, addition, and subtraction. She also improved our reading ability.

I always enjoyed going on school trips, to places like Hacklebarny State Park, where I could stand in the stream's running water, turning over rocks, to look for crayfish. These things looked like miniature lobsters and were as fast as a rocket. Because they had pinching claws, I called them snappers. Many escaped my little hands before I got lucky and caught one. A lesson I learned fast, they could really pinch with their little claws and leave your finger hurting, sometimes dripping a few drops of blood.

My classmates and I always browned-bagged our lunches for these trips. Most of us brought peanut butter and jelly sandwiches on white bread, an apple, and some snacks—there were no peanut allergies back then!

Our class had Mrs. Rooney as our third-grade teacher. She was another great teacher, a gentle soul that we treasured. In this grade, we began learning and memorizing times tables.

Early in our third grade school year, I was told that the school doctor would be coming to give all of us a yearly health physical. I was scared to death of doctors back then.

With one sentence, they could send me off to a hospital where other doctors could knock me out, stick a knife in me, and cut out some part of me.

That dreadful health examination day came without warning. Dr. Powers arrived at our school carrying his black leather bag. I wasn't alone in my fear about getting checked out, many other kids felt the same way. Before long, the whispered rumor reached my classroom. This rumor was confirmed when the intercom blasted and my heart skipped a few beats. "Doctor Powers has arrived. When your class is called, go to room 4." I watched the big clock on the wall, as it clicked minute by minute, dreading my health exam. At precisely 11:20, the intercom blasted, "Mrs. Rooney, send your class to room 4." My heart had been beating at a wild rate before the announcement, and now had gone into overdrive, kettledrumming in my chest.

I wanted to sneak off and hide in a closet, but our teacher made sure we were all accounted for. I stood in line shaking with fear. The line inched up, kid by kid. Gary was standing behind me, his father happened to be a doctor, so he was smart about medical things. I turned and whispered to him, "What's he trying to hear with that snooper scope?"

"He's checking our hearts and lungs, to make sure they're working right. By-the-way, that thing he's using isn't a snooper scope, it's called a stethoscope."

14

With a snicker on his face, Gary added, "He's going to stick that thing on your chest, listen, and hear only one thing inside you—gas circling around in your belly, ready to explode out your backside, buddy!" He placed his hand over his mouth, struggling to hold back laughs.

"Can he really hear stuff like that?" I asked, with an amazed look on my face.

"Yup—everything!"

The kid ahead of me completed his exam and headed back to class. The doctor motioned with his hand for me to stand in front of him. At that point, I was shaking worse than coming out of an ice-cold swimming pool on a windy day. I couldn't get what Gary had said out of my head. *What's he going to hear when he places that scope thing to my chest? I hope, not gas!*

He touched the metal disk on the snooper scope against my chest, and I instantly jumped back from the cold metal, scaring the dickens out of both of us.

"You're not nervous, Greg, are you?"

"Scared out of my wits, Doctor Powers! Can't you see how much I'm shaking? That stetha-thing feels like you stored it in your freezer overnight!"

Ignoring my answer, he placed his left hand on my back and slammed the stetha-thing against my bare chest.

"Take it easy, will you, your heart is beating really fast."

"Like a woodpecker, Dr. Powers? Do you hear anything else circling around in there, like gas?" I asked, looking very worried.

Doctor Powers removed the scope-thing from his ears and let it dangle from his neck, like he was going to answer me. He looked up at me wearing a serious face, put the thing in his ears, didn't answer, and then said, "Breathe in and out deeply, now."

15

"I've been breathing deeply ever since I set foot into this room, Dr. Powers."

"Try again."

Next, the doctor held this odd-looking silver flashlight with a black plastic attachment and was ready to stick it in my ear. I lifted my hand to block the flashlight and said, "You don't have to do that to me, Dr. Powers, I can hear really well." He didn't listen to me that time either and stuck it in both ears anyway.

After he looked in my ears, he threw the plastic thing in the wastebasket.

He then said, "Open your mouth and say ah."

I reluctantly opened my mouth, as he cautiously stuck the huge wooden Popsicle™ stick into my mouth and looked inside with his special flashlight. *You had better not stick that thing in too far, I almost puked in your face last year.* I think he remembered that, as he was careful about how far back to put in the stick. He pulled it out and wrote something in his black spiral notebook.

Dr. Powers turned, looked me straight in my eyes, and said, "Your parents have got to do something about those tonsils."

I immediately started to shake, even more, thinking about having to go to a hospital, to have some doctor cut them out. Then I said back to Dr. Powers, "Please don't tell my parents— I don't want to go to the hospital!" He ignored me once again, looked away, and sent me on my way.

Unfortunately, most parents didn't teach dental hygiene to their children, like brushing your teeth twice a day. One boy in my class bragged that he never brushed his teeth! Sweets were grossly consumed when I was a kid, starting out with highly sugared morning cereals, ice cream and huge sized candy bars at school after lunch, followed by sodas and my favorite, root beer floats when we got home for an afternoon snack. I always liked those ice-cold glass bottles of soda that contained many teaspoons of sugar dissolved in that delicious dark liquid.

Add to all of that, my yearly Easter basket and endless hard candies at Christmas time. No one went to see a dentist until a tooth rotted out from a large cavity. All the kids in my class had cavities because no one supervised what we ate. Parents didn't connect sugar consumption as a cause of cavities, an unknown at the time. Most kids of my era entered adulthood with heavily filled teeth.

We had room mothers in the lower grades to assist teachers. They went on class trips to chaperone, helped on class picnics, and brought special treats to our class on holidays. My mother often volunteered to be one. When the month of June arrived, we had our class picnics. My parents had a large backyard and hosted a few of them. We played games like baseball, badminton, and tag—our favorite. We enjoyed hotdogs, beans and potato salad along with endless soda and ice cream for dessert.

In fourth grade, we had Mrs. Farley as our teacher—one of my favorite teachers. She was one of the teachers that served as a terrific role model growing up. Mrs. Farley loved to tell stories about her family and could spend an entire class period doing so. It didn't take long for my classmates and me to pick up on that. We took advantage of her some days, getting her started on her family, to avoid classwork or a test.

In fifth-grade art, our projects got more complex. Our art teacher introduced us to ceramics and we got to choose an item to make as a project. My classmates and I made ceramic projects to give to our parents as Christmas gifts. The word Christmas could be used freely when I was a kid—Christmas break, Christmas tree, Christmas play were okay to say—political and religious correctness hadn't been thought of yet. I made a pair of ceramic candlestick holders that were formed as stars. I painted them dark green. At the end of class, our teacher collected all our projects to have them glazed in an oven. The next week when she returned, I couldn't believe how beautiful all of these items looked, just like they were made by professionals.

My parents were completely surprised on Christmas morning when they unwrapped the candlestick holders.

When I reached sixth grade, we no longer had one teacher for all of our subjects. We were lucky at Mendham Borough Elementary School to have had wonderful teachers, especially in our lower grades. They served as role models and we held them with high esteem. On Fridays, for our last period, children of the Roman Catholic faith went for religious instruction, while the rest had clubs. The first Friday that happened, I got confused if I was supposed to go with the church kids.

Having religious parents, I knew they would want me to have religious training too, so I joined the Catholic children. I got no religion that day! I ended up making a fool out of myself fiddling around with the holy water then falling on the floor trying to genuflect. I ended up being escorted back to school to Principal Laterlee's office—I was Catholic for only one day, but not a very good one.

When I got that fiasco straightened out, I chose to join the photography club that met in the projection booth on the second floor. This room was dark as night. It had a sink with running water, and all the necessary chemicals to develop the black and white photographic film. To illuminate the room, when we were developing a film, we had a red safelight bulb that hung from the ceiling. There was also a cylindrical tank that we poured chemicals into to develop our film. What was difficult, was getting the right temperature for both the tank's liquid chemical developer and the finishing tray's bath, that completed the developing process.

After we processed the film, it was like magic. We held up a strip of the film next to the bulb and saw the developed pictures. Next, we hung the strips up on a string with clothespins to dry. When we were done, we dumped all the used chemicals down the sink—so much for environmental safety. We never thought about environmental issues then and neither did anyone else. The following week, when we had photography, the filmstrip had dried and was ready to print.

We then used an enlarger to print out our pictures. These photographs were taken with our Kodak™ Brownie™ cameras.

In seventh and eighth-grade, boys had woodshop and girls had home economics. The girls learned how to cook and sew, while the boys learned how to work with wood. Even though I used hand tools building buggies, it would be my first time to use a band saw, drill press, sander, and table saw. But first, I had to learn power tool safety and how to read dimensions from a drawing to build something. My first project was a small kitchen shelf for cookbooks.

Eighth-grade was tough, when our teacher, who we called Mr. A, really confused us in math. My classmates and I thought we mastered all there was to learn in math. We finished off finding the square root and working with exponents and thought we were a bunch of young mathematicians. That thought faded instantly, when one afternoon, Mr. A picked up a piece of white chalk and wrote $20X = 130$.

"Ok class, this was in your homework last night. Any volunteers on how we find what the value of X is?" Mr. A said, without a student responding. "Tom, how about you? How do we solve the problem?"

"Mr. A, I don't haven't a clue."

This challenged most of us, especially when the difficulty increased solving word problems.

My eighth-grade school trip was really special, a trip to Washington, DC. My classmates and I met early one morning to carpool to the train station in Newark. My dad volunteered to drive a station wagon full of anxious kids to the railway station. Most of us, including myself, never traveled by train. It was an exciting moment to climb the steps and board our train. A few minutes later, the conductor shouted, "All aboard!" Then we were on our way, clickety-clack, down the track, to our nation's capital.

Four hours later, we arrived in Washington, D.C., where a bus was waiting to take us to our hotel—a high one with lots of floors.

We got to visit all the important buildings; the Capitol, Washington Monument, Lincoln Memorial, and the White House. Even though our trip was only a few days, kids got homesick.

Then there was the incident—the serious one! Some of the class troublemakers packed balloons in their suitcases to take on the trip. When they bragged about that, I thought they'd fill them with their hot air to celebrate our arrival in Washington—nope, they had a better idea! The masterminds filled the balloons with water and dropped them from five stories up onto unsuspecting adults coming home from work. Note: back then, open windows cooled the hotel rooms.

While our class was eating dinner, the D.C. Police Department was investigating complaints about pedestrians being bombarded with water-balloons. It didn't take the cops long to figure out what floor and room numbers the balloons came from—the ones that Mendham kids occupied. The hotel's management and security detail soon knocked on the troublemakers doors. No, my shared room didn't drop any. Luckily, none of the kids had been led away in handcuffs. However, the day we checked out, we were told that Mendham classes were not welcome to stay at this hotel in the future.

My last memory of Mendham Borough Grammar School was graduation day. I had mixed feelings going around in my head; saying goodbye to a school that had so many good memories, nervous to stand in front of so many people in a packed auditorium, and thinking about what it would be like attending Morristown High School.

I met my classmates in our homeroom with my cap and gown in hand. We slipped them on over our clothes, put on our caps, and placed the tassels on our right side. Our teacher signaled us it was time to go. Reaching the auditorium doorway, we lined up in order and waited.

Then we heard the organist, down in front, starting to play *Pomp and Circumstance,* with my heart kettledrumming to the beat.

I shuffled my feet down the aisle trying to march when I spotted the guy sitting on the organ bench and thought he looked familiar. As we got closer, I was astounded to see it was Principal Latterlee. A thought flashed through my head. *He could not only keep you back, to repeat a grade, with the stroke of his pen, but play the organ, too. Maybe, he was so happy to get rid of my class that he decided to play the organ in celebration of us leaving. One thing for sure, he would never forget the day I was late for school because I was chased up a tree by wild horses and that I was Mischievous in Mendham!*

Chapter 2

Santa Claus and the Chimney

Mendham Borough, New Jersey 1948

In my early childhood, Santa Claus was awesome. His yearly visit was the most exciting part of my life. This would be my sixth Christmas coming up and my excitement had ramped up to an unbelievable level. It was right after Thanksgiving, in November, when the thought of Santa coming on his sleigh landing on our roof dominated my mind. Every day I thought about his elves. I hoped that they were able to make all the toys necessary for all the kids in the world. Then I thought about the reindeer, especially Rudolph. Would he be able to find my house? Every night, I would climb into bed, get under the covers, and drift into sleep thinking about Santa's visit on Christmas Eve. Thoughts rumbled back and forth in my mind: *What if there is no snow? What if the reindeer get sick? What if Santa accidentally skips over my house?*

The next day the *Sears Wish Book*™ Christmas catalog arrived in the mail printed in full color, brilliant colors to be more exact. I was in paradise looking at all the toy trucks, cars, games, Erector™ sets, guns, and even candy. How was I ever going to decide what toys to ask Santa for this Christmas?

Time rolled by quickly until Christmas was three days away. I dreamt that Santa couldn't fit down our chimney. This was the most horrible nightmare of nightmares! The next morning when I woke up, I jumped out of bed and raced down the hall for the living room where our fireplace is located. I removed the protective fire screen and looked up. What did I see? I saw a big hunk of metal closing off the entire fireplace, I yelled, "Oh no!" *There's no way he's going to get his big fat belly and sack of toys down this chimney.*

Immediately, I ran throughout the house calling desperately for my mother.

"Mom, Mom, you've got to come here!"

I found my mother busy cleaning away in the kitchen.

"Mom, Santa's not going to fit down the fireplace!"

She just laughed. A short time later, I grabbed her by the apron and tugged her with all my strength to get her to the living room to see the problem.

"Bend down Mom and see for yourself!"

"That's not a problem," she said.

She moved a lever that made a squeaky noise that opened the chimney; she called it a flue. "See; take look for yourself, it's open."

I crawled on my hands and knees to take a look. "Mom, I see daylight!" Crawling out of the fireplace, I heard my mother mutter silently, "*That solves that problem*."

Looking up at my mom I said, "What do you mean 'that solves that problem?' There's no way Santa is going to get down this hole! Even I won't fit, I'll show you." In a blink of the eye, before my mother could answer me, I was back in the fireplace trying to crawl past the flue. You guessed it, I got stuck.

"Mom! Mom! Get me out of here, I'm stuck!" These words of panic echoed throughout the chimney. Moments later, my mother grabbed me by the legs and pulled my arms and head out of the flue. When I got out, my mother was laughing hysterically.

"This isn't funny! I could have been stuck in there forever!"

"Well, you look so darn funny with your darkened face and hands covered in black soot."

"Mom, I told you; he's not going to fit!"

She grabbed me by the hand and pulled me straight to the bathroom. Every step of the way I jabbered a mile a minute about this awful predicament. Without saying one single word, she lifted me up to face the mirror. What did I see? Two white eyes staring out from a very dark blackface. In utter horror, I turned around and looked at my mom. She burst out laughing.

"What so funny Mom?" It was really scary getting stuck in the fireplace! Santa's not going to get down our chimney!"

"I'm sorry honey, you look really cute. Maybe, I should write a story about this for *Reader's Digest*, the December Christmas issue, next year."

Off came my shirt and pants. My mom pushed my head down into the sink to wash my hair but I thought it was to shut me up. I was still babbling away about Santa when a cup of water came splashing down over my head like a waterfall. She washed my hair with lots of water and shampoo, then washed my face and hands with a washcloth.

As my mom dried me off, I started shivering. She placed a large bath towel around me and marched me to my bedroom to get me dressed. In my bedroom, she pulled out new underwear, jeans, and a white sweater. I'm a big boy now, so I put most of my clothes on myself. Sweaters always give me a problem; I usually get stuck inside putting them on.

"Put your arms up in the air," Mom said. She slipped the sweater over them.

After she combed my hair, I said to her, "Mom, there's no way that Santa will be able to get down our chimney, especially with a bag of toys on his back."

"Sure he'll fit down our chimney, he always does," my mother said.

As my mother's words were rolled out, I looked up at my mother. *How can that be?* I just stared at her. Could my day get any worse?

That's when my world turned upside down. Knowing she was trying to pull the wool over my eyes, I knew I had to use stronger language. I heard men use a special word, damn, to emphasize something; damn weather, damn dog, damn car, and the list went on. So I tried this tactic to bring my mother to her senses.

"Mom! There is no **damn** way that Santa is fitting down this chimney."

After I said that, all hell broke out. My mother grabbed me by my collar, dragged me to the bathroom, off the kitchen, in front of the sink, and said, "Open your mouth."

I was so scared, shaking all over. I had no idea what was to come. She took a bar of Ivory soap™, 99.9% pure, and shoved it into my mouth to make me purer.

She screamed, "You never, ever use that word! It's a bad word!"

I went off screaming, crying my brains out on my way to the kitchen to get a glass of water to rinse my mouth. No matter how many times I rinsed, I couldn't get rid of the taste of soap. I ran off to my bedroom crying.

Later, Mom knocked on my door.

"How about after lunch, I'll take you to see Santa? You can tell him all about our chimney. I'm sure he'll answer all your questions."

After a speedy lunch—I've never eaten so fast in my life—we were on our way to Morristown. We parked on what they call 'The Green.' And there he was, sitting on a tall chair wearing his bright red and white suit and hat. He even had a beard, a really long one, just like all my storybook pictures. I looked around for the reindeer but they must have been somewhere else.

When my mother parked the car, I raced off to see Santa, leaving my mother behind. I raced past all the kids and their mothers that were patiently waiting in line. This act in itself almost caused a parental riot.

Kids started crying and yelling, "No fair, we got here first!"

Their mothers shouted, "Get in line! Wait your turn!"

There was so much commotion, that it got the attention of a nearby cop.

I turned around, faced all the angry mothers and children, and blurted out, "Would you all shut up! I've got a serious problem to discuss with Santa!"

I could see my mother stomping up the sidewalk in great haste to resolve the matter. Before my mother reached me, I shouted, "Santa, I need to talk to you right away, it's really important!"

My mother grabbed my hand and forcibly dragged me away, profusely apologizing to all the other mothers as she took me to the end of the line. It seemed to take forever for my turn to talk to Santa. When Santa's helper—a pretty woman—also dressed in red, said, "Next," I ran to Santa and hopped right up on his lap.

"And what do you want for Christmas?" he asked.

"To warn you about my chimney! You're not going to fit down it!"

"Oh, don't you worry a thing about that."

Out of range for my mother to hear, I whispered, "I'm telling you Santa, there's no damn way you're getting down that damn chimney!"

"And how do you know that?"

"I tried to go up it this morning and got stuck!"

With a loud laugh, Santa asked, "You did what?"

"Santa, this is really important, you have to know this; you won't fit down my chimney. I tried to put my head and arms up into the chimney this morning and got stuck. Look at the size of you and look at me. You're not going to fit. I don't want you stuck and have to call the fire department to get you out. Everyone would see you getting rescued and there would be a lot of kids that would wake up on Christmas morning without toys."

"You've got to go on a diet Santa—right now! This Christmas you have to stop eating cookies at every house. That's a mountain of cookies Santa. No wonder you're so fat!

At this point, more children and mothers had arrived and the line had increased greatly. Santa turned and began whispering in his pretty assistant's ear, "I've got to get rid of this kid. He's a real pain in the ass."

27

Hearing what he said, I replied, "Wait, you're not getting rid of me! I've got more questions to ask you."

"Look what Santa has for you. Here's a nice candy cane—now run along back to your mom."

"No! I want to know how you're going to get into my house to drop off my toys."

"Don't tell me no! You're really driving Santa nuts! Keep acting like this and Santa will not come to your house this year—now get down!"

With tears falling and on the verge of crying, I begged, "But, please Santa, tell me!"

"Now stop the tears. Santa can't tell you all his secrets."

"What are you're going to do if there is no snow on Christmas Eve, Santa?"

Santa was quick with his answer, "My reindeer can fly through the air just like a magic carpet, and they don't need snow." He handed me a candy cane and said, "Go back to your mom, now!"

"No damn way!"

"Does your mother know you talk like this?"

"Yeah, she shoved a damn bar of soap in my mouth this morning!" *The magic word worked, it sure got Santa's attention.*

"One more question, what are you going to do if Rudolph gets sick? If he gets sick, he won't be able to guide your sleigh to anyone's house. Don't worry Santa, I've got an answer. While you're on your diet for the next three days you can spend that time telling Dasher where all the kids' houses are."

At this point, the din on 'The Green' became noisy from all the anxious children wailing in line. Several mothers shouted, "He's been there long enough!" Santa, seeing and hearing all the parental complaints proceeded to remove me from his lap. As he lifted me from his lap, I grabbed on to the first thing I saw to stay put, Santa's beard. A second later, to my amazement, I was holding Santa's beard dangling in my hand. Panic broke out instantly.

Most mothers waiting in line shrieked at the shock of seeing Santa beardless. There were a few mothers, however, that broke out in wild laughter over Santa's dilemma. In a moment's time, mothers shielded their children's view. Some just stood in front of their kids. One mother opened her coat, wrapped it around her child waiting for Santa's beard to be stuck back in place.

Santa and his helper tried to get my prized Santa's beard. But, I was too fast for them. When one of them attempted to grab it; I instantly moved it somewhere else. *Gee, this is really fun, I thought!* One time, I waved it proudly in the air, missing all four hands. It was those two against little me.

"Want your beard back Santa? Tell me how you're going to get inside my house!"

Santa's face glowed red with his eyes nearly popping out of his head. He brought his head up next to my ear and said, "Give me the damn beard."

There's that magic word again.

Then I got a great idea, I sat on it. Both of them froze. They just stared at me.

Santa said to the helper, "Well what are you waiting for—get the beard!"

"Not on your life—I'm not grabbing it there."

Santa grabbed my arm, squeezing it hard, and held one end of the beard. The helper grabbed my hand holding the beard and began unwrapping each of my fingers, one by one. I glanced up to look at beardless Santa. He wasn't looking at me at all. He just stared at his attractive helper, with a big grin on his face.

He whispered to her, "I wish you were sitting on my lap instead of this brat!"

Why would Santa want her on his lap? Is she going to tell Santa what she wants for Christmas?

Just as the helper got to my last two fingers, I slipped my other three free ones back to grab the beard. In complete frustration, she said in a quiet voice to Santa, "I can't get the damn beard out of his hand."

There's that magic word again, I thought.

Seeing the disaster at hand, the cop and my mother were both on their way to handle the situation. The cop arrived first and said in a firm voice, "Let go of the beard and get off of Santa's lap!" I was scared as hell—one of my older brother's pet words—and dropped the beard, right on the ground. Santa's helper picked up the beard and secured it somehow back onto Santa. My mother stood in front of me staring at me with a stern, unhappy scowling expression. Grabbing my hand, she whisked me roughly off Santa's lap.

"Wait till we get home! You're going to be grounded for two weeks! You'll be lucky if you get coal in your stocking for Christmas!"

Before my mother could pull me away from Santa, I yelled; "You didn't answer my question! How are you going to get your fat ass down my damn chimney?"

It was shortly thereafter, my mother gave me a few hard smacks on my ass before we got to the car.

On the way back to Mendham, I feared the soap punishment. I said to my mom, "Well that was a wasted trip! Santa didn't answer my questions."

Mom said, "Answer your questions, you're lucky that the policeman didn't arrest you and put you in jail!"

"Mom, policemen don't arrest kids, especially not three days before Christmas."

"Do you know what Santa said to me?"

"No, what did he tell you, Mom?"

"Never bring that kid back here again."

"Don't blame me, blame that fake Santa. If he were the real Santa, he would have told me how he was going to get into our house, then, none of this would have ever happened. And, I wouldn't have been able to pull his beard off.

We pulled into the driveway and mom parked the car. My mother was not in a good mood at all. To say the least, she was very angry at me.

"You go straight to your room! I don't want to hear a peep out of you! Wait till your father gets home tonight!"

It was about six in the evening when my dad got home from a business trip. He came in through the front door, gave my mother a big hug, and said, "What's new?"

My mother said, "I don't know where to begin."

The next three days took forever, especially grounded in my room. I was so excited on Christmas morning to see an Erector Set™ in a huge red metal case sitting under the tree and my red Christmas stocking hung on the fireplace mantle. I ran to the stocking first and peeked inside—no coal! It was filled with all sorts of candy, Crayons, and a big navel orange.

When my parents went to have breakfast in the kitchen, I quietly opened the fireplace screen to check out the chimney. I looked up the chimney and to my amazement, there was a paper note taped to the opened flue. I yanked it off and read it.

"I GOT MY BIG ASS THROUGH. MERRY CHRISTMAS, SANTA."

A letter from Santa! He's got to be real!

Later in the morning, around ten, our family relatives started to arrive at our home. It was my parent's tradition to serve coffee, tea, coffee cake, and cookies to our guests. Everyone had finished their morning coffee and tea; it was time to exchange presents. I sat on the floor and watched as we went around the room taking turns opening them up. My Aunt Holly's turn was coming up next. She goes crazy about celebrating Christmas; maybe it's because of her name. She makes a real fuss when she opens her presents too—shrieking and kissing everyone. My father says, "She's a real pain in the butt, a real fusspot about what she gets for gifts."

My mother got our present for Aunt Holly from under the tree and handed it to her. It was in a big box, decorated with a bright red ribbon.

As she started to open it, her thoughts came to me as clear as a bell. *This must be something really nice. I can't wait to see what it is.* She smiled from ear to ear. As she ripped the paper off and stared at the box, it read in big letters, **FOOT MASSAGER.** She kept turning the box over and over. Each side read, **FOOT MASSAGER.** I noticed her smile disappear more and more each time she turned the box. She wasn't happy. With a disappointed look on her face, she set her gift on the rug.

I knew exactly what she was thinking, *What am I ever going to do with this piece of crap?* I couldn't hold back anymore, I broke out in hysterical laughter. I rolled around laughing uncontrollably. The words flew out of my mouth, "A piece of crap!" When I finally stopped laughing, I looked around the room and saw no one was laughing, including my Aunt.

Looking up at her, she got a disgusted look on her face. Her eyes glared down at me. Turning, she looked at my mother and said, "What's wrong with him? He acts so strangely at times."

Chapter 3

The Easter Bunny

Mendham Borough, New Jersey 1949

Before I knew it, Easter was almost here, only three days away. Still amazed at how Santa got down the chimney, I got thinking about the Easter Bunny.

How was he going to get in our house?

It was Friday morning. My parents called it Good Friday. I don't know why they called it that. All the other Fridays are just plain Fridays. It must have something to do with the Easter Bunny coming in three days.

I got back to playing with my Erector Set™. It has a book to show you how to build a lot of neat stuff or you can use your imagination to build anything you want. I just built a crane using metal parts and screws in the set all by myself. It's ready to lift my little toy truck now.

"Breakfast is ready!" My mother shouted from the other side of the house.

"I'm coming!" I walked into the kitchen and there was Mom; she looked at me with a big grin.

"Your favorite," she said.

"Looks really yummy, Mom!"

After I ate a few spoons of cereal, I decided to have a serious conversation with her. "Mom, remember back on Christmas morning, the note I found in the chimney stuck on the flue?

"Yes, the one from Santa."

"I still don't know how he got down our chimney. How does the Easter Bunny get into our house each year?"

"Every year he finds his way in. I'm sure Sunday morning you'll find an Easter Basket filled with eggs and candy waiting for you."

"Seriously Mom, I've got to know how he gets in our house."

"Why don't you ask your father? I'll leave him to discuss this with you."

"But, Mom!"

"Eat your breakfast and stop bugging me! I don't want to go through this ordeal we had to go through last Christmas. Do you realize, you're the only kid banned from ever coming back to see Santa on 'The Green' in Morristown?"

As I ate my breakfast, I analyzed the big mystery—analyze is one of my father's favorite words. When Mom has some sort of a problem, he always tells her, "I've got to analyze the problem first." But, I know what he's really thinking in his head, "*that will shut her up for a while.*"

Well back to analyzing. Hopping up on the roof and down the chimney route won't work for the Easter Bunny. He doesn't have reindeer like Santa, so flying through the sky won't work either. Maybe he comes in through one of the doors. That would mean that Mom or Dad would have to leave a door open all night. I closed my eyes and thought about last Easter. *We never opened a door last year. That's not it. There's only one other way he can get in, an open window. I don't see how that would work either. He may be too big to fit through the window opening. This analyzing is giving me a headache.*

There had to be a simple explanation. Bingo! I'll hide in the living room and catch him in the act. This will solve the Easter Bunny mystery once and for all. Better yet, I'll capture him. That would make me famous. Can you imagine the huge headline in our local newspaper? **Mendham Boy Captures Easter Bunny.** *Come to think of it, it might even make the WOR radio news with Paul Harvey. Mom and Dad always listen to him.*

Now, how am I going to catch him? Does he hop or run? All the pictures of him in magazines have him standing on two legs.

34

I never saw a real rabbit do that though. Well, I could set a trap, but that's no good—I don't want to hurt him. I don't have a trap anyway. Got it! I'm going to lasso him just like the Lone Ranger lassoes bad guys. I'll have to aim high to get the lasso over those tall ears though. Where am I going to find a rope? Mom's clothesline! That will make a great lasso and give me lots of extra rope to tie him up.

Saturday morning I got up really early to take Mom's clothesline down. Dressed in my pajamas, I quietly slipped out the back door to get a stepladder from the barn. The ladder was too heavy for me to lift so I had to drag it all the way to the house and quietly up the back steps. After I opened the ladder and placed it under the pulley on the floor; I tried to unhook the clothesline. I tugged and pulled with all my strength, but it didn't come off. After several tries, I gave up. *I'll just cut the rope—problem solved!*

I shot down the ladder, headed for the kitchen and got a sharp knife. Up the ladder I went and cut the rope. Moments later, the rope fell to the ground. Easing the ladder down, I dragged it back to the barn. On the way over to the barn, the thought came to me. *What if Mom needs to hang out wash today?*

I ran back to, got the rope and hid it under some bushes so my mom and dad wouldn't see it.

Slipping back into the house, I tip-toed to my bedroom and got under the covers. I had just got back to sleep when a drawer slammed shut in my parent's room and woke me up—their room is next to mine.

Then, the toilet flushed, a good sign that my mom and dad had gotten up. Several minutes later, I heard my mom yawn as she and Dad walked past my bedroom door. Mom asked Dad, "What's the weather going to be today?"

"It's going to be nice, sunny in the sixties."

"A good day to wash before Easter Sunday," Mom said.

What luck! My mom either had to dry our wash on the rope in the basement or outside on the clothesline.

35

No question about it, she's going for the outside line today. She likes the outdoor smell, as fresh as a daisy, she always says.

"Oh no!" *I hope this will not turn out to be another Ivory soap™ day for me.* If they figure out I did it, Mom will tell Dad to discipline me. That's a word I really hate. Dad doesn't use the Ivory soap™ punishment, he just thinks of idiotic jobs for me to do. My last punishment was last Saturday. I had to wash the family car. Well, let me tell you what happened.

Dad drove his car up to the house for me to wash. He was all dressed up in his best Sunday clothes. Dad was taking Mom out for a fancy dinner. Mom had arranged for Mary, a high schooler, to come over and take care of me, to make sure I didn't get into any mischief.

"I'll be back in a minute," he said.

He came out the back door with a pail of hot soapy water and a long-handled brush and set it down at my feet. He was being very careful not to soil his good clothes. Dad likes to do everything neatly. Mom said he's a real fusspot, just like my Aunt Holly.

Dad said, "This is how you wash a car." First, you wet it all down, soap it up, and then rinse the soap off. Always start at the top and work your way down. Come here, I want to show how to use a water nozzle. See this lever, when you squeeze it, water comes out here."

"Just like a giant water gun, Dad."

"Forget that idea! It's not a water gun. Okay, now let's get started, your mom and I have to leave soon to go out for dinner. I'll stay here and watch you for a while to make sure you do it right."

"Like this Dad?"

"You forgot to do that window."

With the water squirting full blast, I turned around to ask my father which one and ended up drenching him.

My father yelled, "Shut the damn water off!"

There's that magic word again, I thought.

"Put everything down and go back into the house!"

"What about my punishment?" My father looked down at his drenched suit, looked at me, and gave me an angry look.

He walked over to the water faucet on the house and shut it off.

Just then, my mother came out the back door, looked all around for my father, and shouted, "Walt, are you ready to go yet?"

Peeking out the kitchen window, I saw my dad walk over to where my mom could see him and said, "Not really!"

Mom said, "Why were you washing the car with your good clothes on? You knew we were going out for dinner!"

That did not turn out to be a good afternoon for anyone. Mom and Dad had 'words' with each other and both were mad at me. Well, that was how that punishment worked out.

Early the next morning, I was down on the floor playing with my Erector Set™ crane, lifting my little toy truck up and down when the thought came to me; *the Easter Bunny is coming tomorrow, got to practice using a lasso.* My thought about the bunny ended when Mom yelled from the kitchen.

"Breakfast is ready!"

Scared to death about the clothesline, I took my time to get to the kitchen for breakfast. I felt as guilty as a bandit and held my head down to avoid looking at Mom. On Saturday mornings, we always have a hot breakfast. At my place setting, was a stack of blueberry pancakes with maple syrup dripping down over the edges. As we ate, I glanced up now and then at my mom eating her breakfast. Out of nowhere, she said, "You look kind of sheepish today."

"What do you mean, I look sheepish? You don't see me with four legs and a tail do you?"

37

"You don't look like a sheep! You just don't seem yourself. You usually shovel your pancakes down and ask for more."

I had just started to swallow a mouthful of pancakes—timing is everything—when Mom said, "got to get a load of wash started." The pancakes got stuck halfway down my throat like they were glued. I started to choke, grabbed my glass of milk, and took a big gulp to wash them down. *It's only a matter of time now until Mom discovers the clothesline missing. This might be another Ivory soap™ day for me.* I felt sick to my stomach, got up from the table, scraped my breakfast pancakes into the garbage, ran to my bedroom, and slammed the door shut.

Feeling sick to my stomach, I flopped down on my bed hoping this situation would go away. All of a sudden, Mom screamed:

"The clothesline's gone!"

Clomp, clomp, clomp; my mother's footsteps headed up the hall, right for my room. *Should I hide under the bed? No, I'll just play the innocent little boy, which works sometimes.* My door swung open and slammed against the wall. Mom stood there with her arms on her hips and looked down at me on the floor, really angry. *She's pissed—one of my dad's descriptions of my mom when she gets really mad.*

"Did you take my clothesline?"

"No, I've been playing in my room since I got up, Mom."

I knew what she was thinking.

Yeah, sure you have. Tell me another story. Her thoughts came blasting into my head.

"Hand over the clothesline—now!"

"Don't have it, Mom." The thought came to me to tell her the Easter Bunny might have taken it, but didn't want to push my luck, and played my innocent little boy game. She turned and headed out of my room, probably to find my dad.

"Walt! Walt! The clothesline has been stolen!"

"Now Jan, who would steal our clothesline?" My dad asked. "I'll drive to the hardware store and get you a new one."

A short time later, there was my dad on the stepladder stringing the new rope through the house pulley. As he finished running the rope through the second pulley, Mom stood on the back steps with her wet wash, ready to hang it out.

After lunch, Mom came to my room and said, "Your father and I are going to Morristown to do some shopping. Mary is here, she will look after you."

Oh, fiddly sticks! I thought.

My Mom and Dad began to walk out of the house, as Mom shouted, "Stay out of trouble!"

As soon as their car disappeared out of the driveway, I ran outside to get the rope from under the bushes. Mary was in the living room studying for a test, nowhere in sight, so I grabbed the rope and headed to the barn. She never goes there. She saw a big black snake there once while she was caring for me and never has gone back since. On the way there, the thought came to me. *How big is the Easter Bunny?*

I slid the barn door open and looked around for something the size of the bunny to lasso. Right in front of me was a big bale of hay. *That'll work.* I pulled it outside on the lawn, set it on end, and headed back to the barn for something for the head. *There's a steel pail, that'll work.* I brought it outside and placed it upside down on top of the bale of hay. At the end of the rope I made a lasso; then, swirled it around my head, and let it go. Bang! The pail got knocked to the ground.

It took me forever to learn how to lasso the pail. But then, with each throw, the lasso landed around the hay bale. *I'd better put everything away before they get back.* I pulled the bale of hay back into the barn, where Dad had stored it. My father was like a detective, he noticed anything out of place. Carefully, I coiled the rope inside the pail, headed back to my bedroom, and hid the pail of rope in my clothes closet under a spare blanket.

Back on the floor, I got tired of playing with the crane. You can only lift and lower a toy truck for so long. Piece by piece, I took the crane apart. *What am I going to build?* Soon, I just started grabbing the parts and bolting them together; before long, standing on the floor in front of me, was a miniature animal cage.

As I sat there and admired my latest project, I heard my parent's car pull up to the house. We have a circular driveway in front of our house. It connects to a long driveway that goes back to the barn where my dad keeps our car and Farmall™ tractor.

The front door opened and I heard my Mom's footsteps; clomp, clomp, clomp. She was headed to my room. She stopped at my almost closed door and peeked through. I can see her one eye spying on me through the crack. Her eye looks just like a lobster's eye. *She's ready to come down on me for doing something wrong, I just know it. I'm sure the missing clothesline is still fresh in her head, driving her crazy. She knows I took it, but can't prove it. Watching all those detective programs, especially "Man Against Crime" with my dad made me smart about hiding evidence.*

She opened the door and said, "Soooo, have you been a good little boy while we were away?"

"Sure Mom, just sitting here and playing with my Erector Set™."

"What's that you built with all the little metal bars?"

"It's a cage Mom, can't you see that?"

"What are you going to put in the cage? Don't get any bright idea of catching a snake or something outside and putting it in there."

I wanted to tell her it's to hold a small make-believe Easter Bunny prisoner, but thought I better not—I have to keep my plan a secret ."A circus tiger," I said.

Just then, Mary arrived at my bedroom doorway and looked in.

40

"Did he stay out of trouble while we were away?" Mom asked.

"He played outside in the backyard near the barn all afternoon."

Satisfied, Mom and Mary walked away. On the floor, I started to think of my plan to capture the Easter Bunny. The more I thought about it, the more excited I became. *Only hours to go and I'll be famous,* **Mendham Boy Captures Easter Bunny!**

After dinner, Dad and I went out to the den to watch a show on our black and white Dumont™ TV. Not many families in our town have a television. Our family used to listen to only radio programs; you had to use your imagination for them. My favorite radio program was the *Lone Ranger*. With the new television, I don't have to use my imagination anymore. I see everything, right there on the TV screen!

Dad turned on the television. While it warmed-up, we saw a huge white picture with black bars going up and down. He turned a knob to tune the station in. The picture cleared up with a guy standing up telling jokes. Dad thinks he's really funny.

Who is that man, Dad?"

"That's Bob Hope."

"He's not funny to me, Dad. I'm going to my room to play."

When I got to my room, I opened my closet and lifted the folded blanket on top of the pail with the rope. *Soon I'll have that rope around the bunny. It will be sad when I do catch him, he won't be able to talk to me. Rabbits don't talk or make any noise from their mouths. How am I going to ask him how he got in our house if he can't talk? Maybe, I can look through my books to see how rabbits talk to one another.*

I started going through my bookshelves. Mom and dad like to buy me lots of books, they say it will make me a good reader someday and make me smart. In a hurry to find a book about the Easter Bunny, I started checking each book cover on the first shelf. If the book didn't have something about the Easter Bunny or rabbits, I tossed it on the floor.

Soon, the floor was scattered with books—a real mess. Only two more shelves for me to check-out. I was on my last shelf when I found three *Brer Rabbit* books.

I sat on the floor, leaned against my bed, and skimmed through the pages in the books looking at all the pictures of *Brer Rabbit*. He wasn't the Easter Bunny but maybe it would make me smart about rabbits. But, most important, tell me how big the Easter Bunny is. As I got near the end of the last book Mom knocked on my door.

"Yes, Mom."

Mom opened my door and said, "Oh my God, what are you doing? What a mess!"

"I'm reading about rabbits, Mom."

"Why are you so interested in rabbits?"

"To see how big the Easter Bunny is. Haven't found him yet, just found *Brer Rabbit*."

"It's time for bed. Put all these books away and be quick about it."

"Okay, Mom." It took me forever to get all the books back on the shelves. It was almost 8:30 when I slid the last book on the shelf. I got my pajamas on, went to the bathroom, and jumped in bed. Between the big round moon that glowed through my window and the excitement of capturing the Easter Bunny, I couldn't fall asleep. I jumped down from my bed, closed the blinds, and got back under the blanket. Soon, I fell fast asleep.

Creek! I woke up instantly, sat-up in bed, and listened. Creek, Creek! The noise was coming from the living room. *It's got to be the Easter Bunny!* I slipped out of bed, opened the closet and grabbed my lasso. After opening my bedroom door, I crawled down the hall to the living room. As I got to the doorway, there was a shadow bent over placing something near the fireplace. I stood up and quietly slipped into the living room with the lasso in my hand. I spun the lasso around a few times and, let it go.

Whoosh, it went, right over the Easter Bunny. I pulled the rope with all my might so he couldn't get away. *Got him.* The bunny instantly fell over backward.

"What the hell is going on?" my father screamed!

"Is that you, Dad?"

"Of course it's me! Dad grabbed the rope and slipped it off.

The living room light came on. My mother stood there laughing her brains out.

"I guess this will be the last year for the Easter Bunny!" she announced.

I was trying to figure out what she meant by that.

She walked over to the rope, picked it up and said, "My clothesline! That's my missing clothesline!"

Ivory soap™ time again, I thought.

"Dad, what are you doing with my Easter Basket? That's for me, not you! Where's the Easter Bunny?" My brain was going crazy trying to make sense of why Dad was holding the empty Easter basket with all the goodies dumped on the floor. Then, the thought came to me. "Dad, are you the Easter Bunny?"

"There is no Easter Bunny," Mom said. You're old enough now to tell you the truth—it's all a fantasy."

No Easter Bunny. "Oh no! There's a Santa Claus, isn't there?"

"Honey, some people believe there's a Santa Claus," Mom said.

"Think about it, reindeer on the roof, Santa going down our tiny chimney—there's no Santa either, son."

Dad took my prized lasso, coiled it up, and handed it to my mother. "Here is your stolen clothesline, Jan."

"Well, I'll let the Easter Bunny get on with his duties while I get back to bed and go to sleep," Mom said, as she walked back to their bedroom.

I went back to my room, laid face down on my bed and cried, "No Easter Bunny, No Santa." *What am I going to do? My life is ruined! I don't want to live without Santa!* I fell asleep sometime later. In my head, I heard my mom's words. *Some people believe there's a Santa. I'm going to be one of those people. I want him to visit me each year, even if I'm a hundred years old.*

Chapter 4

Jessie & James:

Terror on Four Legs

Mendham Borough, NJ 1950

Jessie and James were not only the names of infamous bank robbers but also the names of two horses that lived next door to us in Mendham. They belonged to the De Groot family, whose property paralleled ours. A tall ten-foot hedge with driveways on each side divided the properties. The neighbor's horses were kept either in the twin open stalls or out in the pasture to graze during the day. The pasture bordered the front area of my parent's property.

Dr. De Groot was a veterinarian who specialized in equestrian medicine. His income came from treating racehorses. His son, Jimmy, about my age, was another great pal that I played with. When we played together, we only played in my yard and that was for a good reason—the horses! Jessie and James did not have a good reputation, much like the infamous bank robbers. They were nasty horses and I was fearful of them. I have no idea what breed they were, but they were retired racehorses that towered above me as an eight-year-old.

My first horrible experience with the horses came when I had taken a shortcut on my way home from school. This was my first day back to school after a major snowstorm. To get home, I took a shortcut through the De Groot's property. I walked up the graveled driveway with snowplowed banks on each side. As I reached near the end of the driveway, about fifty feet from the horse stalls, I hesitated to take another step closer. Jessie and James were in their stalls. A warning floated around in my head. *Don't get any closer.* Then I thought, *just a couple more steps.* I took them.

Jessie and James became aware of my presence and literally went crazy! Maybe I startled them having an afternoon nap. They loudly roared and trumpeted, kicking their stalls trying to break free. They slammed into the retaining rope that was strung loosely across each of their stalls.

It must have been my survival instinct. Scared out of my wits, I jumped over the neighbor's snowbank and dove through the tall hedge to get to my yard. After getting through and getting up, I tried to run, but couldn't. With each step, my legs plunged through the deep snow, slowing me down to a crawl, like running in slow motion. I kept glancing back to make sure the horses hadn't broken loose and were on my trail. If they did, they would probably trample me to death.

I finally reached our steps and ran up them to the back door. I could still hear the angry horses carrying on, kicking their stalls, and loudly trumpeting. From that day on, that experience burned a horrible memory in my brain, never to be forgotten. One day, I asked my Dad why the neighbor's horses hated me so much.

"It's not you. Jessie and James are just high-strung racehorses. They're stallions that have minds of their own, and they're tough to handle. At times they get ornery not having a mare or two to play around with."

"Why don't they just play with one another, Dad?"

"The stallions would fight one another to see which one is stronger. Jessie and James worked that out long ago, with Jessie the winner. They're just in need of a mare or two, to nuzzle up to."

"What's a mare, Dad?"

"A girl horse."

"Well, you better tell that to Dr. De Groot. He better get a herd of mares to get those guys into a better mood!"

****

It was almost Easter break, and I was getting excited about having the week off to do some more experimenting with electronics. I hoped that Dad wouldn't lose any more hair if something went wrong with one of my projects going up in smoke. I heard the back door bell ring and went to see who was at the door. There was my pal, Jimmy, holding a softball in his hand. "Hi Jimmy, good to see you."

"Want to play catch?" he asked.

"Sure, let me put on my sneakers."

"I've got some bad news to tell you, Greg. My dad is changing jobs and we're moving to Florida."

"Oh no! That stinks! I'm going to miss playing with you."

"It sure does. I'll lose you as a friend and I'll have to go to a new school, too," Jimmy said.

"The only pals you're going to have down there buddy, are a bunch of alligators! How soon are you moving?"

"We're going down during my Easter break to find a house and move there in July."

"Who's going to take care of the horses?"

"You are! No, just joshing you. Your brother, Walter, said he'd do it."

"He better be holding his .38, to knock some sense into those two crazy horses."

"Let's toss a few over there. I'll give you some grounders and pop-ups," Jimmy said.

We enjoyed our time together tossing the ball back and forth, but we were also sad, that we'd soon lose our friendship.

It was about six in the evening when I saw Mendham's police car drive past our house. I shot out the back door and ran to talk to my brother, Walter. He hit the brakes, skidding to a stop, and glanced over my way. He opened the door and got out.

47

"Hi, Walter! I've got really bad news—the De Groots are moving."

"Yeah, Doc De Groot got a really good job offer, he couldn't refuse it. They plan to move in July."

"Jimmy told me that they're going to fly down to Florida on his Easter break to look for a new home. He also mentioned that you're going to take care of those two nasty horses, Jessie and James—are you crazy? Those horses will kill you! How are you ever going to get near their stalls? I can't even get within fifty feet without them going berserk!"

"You've got to show them whose boss."

"Good luck with that! Aren't you afraid of getting squashed walking into their stalls?"

"You're right, at fifteen-hundred pounds; they could pin and crush you against the wall, probably killing you. Doc showed me what to do. He's got a hayfork with five very sharp metal points on the end with a short two-foot handle on the other side to take into the stall. If one of the horses tries to squeeze you, you just put the fork sideways between the horse and the stall wall. A few pokes in his side and he learns his lesson, real fast."

"I still wouldn't go in without your .38 if I were you," I warned.

****

It was a nice afternoon, a good time to take a bicycle ride around our yard with my new JC Higgins™ bike, the one I had received for Christmas. It was neat; it had chrome fenders, headlight, and carry rack, along with a maroon frame. The bike had large balloon tires with white pinstriping. In addition, it had a metal body attached to the frame with three fancy air intake vents, just like the Buick™ cars had.

I had gotten the bike out of the barn, jumped on the seat, and peddled at cruising speed. I biked past my brother and his wife's house towards mine. As I got past the front of my house, I made a left to go around our circle driveway and nearly peed my pants when I saw what was standing on our front lawn. I hit the brakes, stopped, and stood straddling my bike, standing perfectly still. There they were, Jessie and James, eating our grass—they had gotten loose. Jessie lifted his head, flipped his main over to the other side, and swished his tail. *What am I going to do? I know they're going to charge me—I just know it. There's no tree close by that I can climb. If there were, they'd probably pull me down by my pants before I got up to safety.*

Jessie lowered his head and gave me an angry look with evil lurking in his eyes. He headed in my direction, swishing his tail, with James following close behind. I dropped my bike and ran as fast as I could through our open porch and up the five cement block steps to the front door. I threw open the outside screen door and tried to turn the front doorknob—locked! *It's never locked. Damn, damn, damn.* I rang the bell, hammered my fist against the solid door, and yelled, "Help! Mom! Open the door! They're after me!" I screamed repeatedly at the top of my lungs.

I turned around, hoping that the horses wouldn't enter the open front porch. This was part of our house and not a barn or stall. I was wrong with that thought! Jessie, being such a big horse, a zillion hands high, ducked his head down and came inside the porch following my path to the stairs, just like a bloodhound. *What am I going to do? He's going to attack me! Trample me to death!* I quickly opened the screen door and sandwiched myself between it and the solid door, placing my feet sideways on the door sill. I was facing Jessie. I held onto the doorknob tight, to keep me in place and balanced on the doorsill. Jessie stared at me through the screen, probably thinking, *I see you, you can't hide from me!*

He probably wants to get even with me for waking him up that other day.

Jessie just stood there with his wild evil eyes, deciding how to take me down. *Where's the FBI when you need them?* My heart was racing and beads of sweat poured out of my skin from head to toes. One thought bounced around in my head.

Maybe he doesn't know how to go up the stairs. I'll bet they didn't teach him that at racetrack school. Jessie proved me wrong. He walked closer and took his first step with ease, without breaking his stare. Soon, he took another step, as if he'd walked up stairs all his life. I stiffened up and pushed myself firmly against the thick door, trying to be as flat as a pancake. I hoped and prayed that Mom would come to open the damn door.

I couldn't get at the bell anymore, so I took my free hand and banged like crazy on the door again, but not with enough force because there was so little room to move my hand. I screamed again for my mom—nothing! *Where was she?* She didn't come! Jessie took another step, then another, all the while his eyes focused on me. I took my other hand and grabbed the screen door handle to help keep it shut—my only protection. I held the door so tight against my face, that my nose got squished into the screen. I hoped by doing that, Jessie wouldn't bite off a piece of my nose along with a mouthful of the screen.

Jessie had put his head right up to the screen, turned it this way and that way, biting at the screen. I felt his hot breath on my face and smelled the fresh grass, he had just eaten earlier. He was so close that I couldn't focus my eyes to see him clearly, but maybe that's a good thing. In my blurred vision, I saw his gigantic stained teeth as he gnawed at the screen. I felt his saliva as it penetrated through the screen onto my nose. As he turned his head to the side, our eyes met once more, but closer this time. I saw my reflection in his dark brown eye. He stomped his feet again, his horseshoes made a loud clatter as they slammed against the cement stair landing.

He continued to try to get at me. I felt his hairy lips against my nose, lips, and forehead. He had not given up. James was standing in the back of him, probably waiting for his turn. Jessie's stomps had gotten more aggressive, as one hoof connected with the bottom of the screen doorframe; the piece broke off and dropped to the landing.

I feared for my life, my sweaty grip on the doorknob became difficult, tired after holding it like a vise for so long. My mind played tricks on me, too.

A vision of the front page of the *Morristown Daily Record* suddenly dropped down like a movie screen in my mind. I nearly fainted after I read the front-page headline, **MENDHAM BOY GETS TRAMPLED TO DEATH!** My mind returned to reality when I heard my mother's footsteps coming to the door. I heard the door lock click open. Mom pulled the door open and saw a huge horse in front of her ready to charge into the house. He saw my mother too! He stomped his front hooves against the landing as he neighed and trumpeted, and he shook his head in anger over not being able to complete his goal—to kill me! My mother stood frozen in fear. She looked like she was ready to faint. I pushed past her and slammed the thick door shut. "We're safe!" I shouted.

She came to her senses and said, "What should we do, call the police?"

"You forgot, Mom, Walter is the police! If anyone knows what to do, he will; he's brave and smart. And if worse comes to worst, he's got a .38 belted to his waist."

Mom, picked up the telephone and heard two women conversing—we have a party line. My dad, called it 'a pain in the ass line.' "Please, this is an emergency! I need to call the police!" Mom said, as the other women politely hung-up their telephones.

[The community of Mendham, being a small country town, had a limited number of telephone lines. This limited the number of private telephone lines that Bell Telephone™ could offer to customers. To solve this problem, Bell Telephone offered customers party line service, whereas many as five homes had to share a single telephone line. If someone was using the line, you had to hang-up and try again later to reach an operator.]

With urgency, she tapped down on the metal telephone hanger several times to signal the switchboard operator.

"How may I help you?" the Mendham operator asked.

"Put me through to the police—it's an emergency! I have two wild horses on my front porch trying to break-in!"

"Mrs. Smith, are you feeling okay?" the operator asked with concern.

"Please! They just tried to kill my son!" She held the line.

"Go ahead, I've got you connected."

"Mendham Borough Police, Chief Smith, speaking."

"Walter! It's your mom, you've got to get here really quick. The De Groot's horses tried to kill Greg and they're both on the front porch trying to break-in the house!"

"I'm on my way!"

With the police station a mile away, we knew he would arrive soon. With our faces glued to the front window, we waited for him. A few minutes later, he came zooming up the driveway with the siren blasting and the red and blue lights flashing. He stepped out with a shotgun in his hand, and opened the trunk and pulled out an emergency road flare. He lit it as blinding sparks flew-out in every direction and walked to the porch. When the horses saw the threatening flare, they freaked out and ran off the porch for their turf, the pasture. Walter followed them, making sure they wouldn't come back. Satisfied, he walked back to the police car to store the shotgun and threw the flare on our gravel driveway. Mom opened the front door to let Walter come inside.

"Gee, they did a number on the screen door and chipped the stairs to pieces," Walter said to us. "You'd better call Doc tonight and tell him he's got to do something with those horses."

"I'm going to let your dad handle that—he's very good at dealing with difficult situations. Oh boy, this evening he's going to go nuts when he hears the horses almost killed Greg. The icing on the cake will be when he sees what happened to his new screen door he just put up last weekend."

"Yeah, he might have Doc served with a restraining order on the horses."

"Walter, may I have one of those flares? It might be a good accessory to add to my new bike in case this happens again. I could use the flare to chase Jessie and James to the haunted barn and let the ghost take care of them. They'd never come in our yard ever again!"

"No—they're too dangerous, you could lose your eye sight or get a serious burn."

It must have been my dad's little chat with Dr. De Groot, but soon after the incident, the horses where gone—thank God! The bad news two months later, so was my pal, Jimmy.

Chapter 5

The New Year's Eve Shooting

Mendham Borough, NJ 1951

Thanksgiving had come and gone and I knew that the *Sears Christmas Wish Book*™ Catalog would soon arrive. So each day after school, I walked into the US Post Office, located near Mendham Borough Grammar School and checked our mailbox. It had one of those small dial locks. I opened the box and anxiously looked for a package notice inside, the one that informed you that your parcel had arrived. If you got one, you had to present it to the clerk that staffed the postal service window to collect it.

I had a feeling in my head that our *Sears Christmas Catalog* might have arrived. I grabbed the stack of envelopes in my hand and fingered through them one by one, looking for the little piece of paper. Near the end of the stack, there it was. I stuffed the envelopes back in the box and rushed over to the clerk. He peered down at me as he took my note and headed to the back of the room to fetch our parcel. At the window, I got up on my toes and shifted around trying to get a better view of what he picked up from the pile. It wasn't a box and looked about the size of a catalog.

"Here you go, young fellow," he said, with a big smile.

I quickly grabbed the package with the large Sears label.

"Thank you, sir," I said, as I walked to the corner of the post office and sat down on the floor. With great excitement, I ripped off the cover and thumbed through the *Christmas Wish Book*™, the section for older kids, like me, a fourth-grader. The catalog pages were in brilliant color that almost made things look real, they almost popped out at you.

This section had Gilbert Erector Sets™, chemistry sets, a ceramic architectural building kit, wood-burning irons, and many things that would make great presents. They even had a section on guns.

From watching cowboy shows, like *Roy Rogers, Gene Autry*, and my favorite, the *Lone Ranger*, I was all psyched-up on asking my parents for a toy gun for Christmas. What added to my need to have one was seeing my brother, Walter, Mendham's Police Chief, carrying a revolver on his belt every day. Thumbing through the pages, I saw twenty-two gauge rifles, B-B, and pellet guns. I knew it would be useless to ask for any of those because Dad would veto every single one of them. There on page 172 was a cork gun. It looked like a real gun. I read the description; the part that drew my attention was that it could knock over a tin can at twenty feet.

Then the thought flashed through my mind, *I've been going to Sunday school every Sunday learning about being a good Christian with peace, love, and joy. And, here I am, wanting a gun for Christmas, the holiday that celebrated Jesus' birth. Should I or shouldn't I ask for a gun?* As fast as this thought entered my mind, it flew out a second later.

Excitement ran through my veins thinking about how much fun I could have with a cork gun, especially with my pals, Al and Sam. Our war battles would take on a new dimension of realism fighting off the Germans. We played this scenario often using Murgatroy, their parents 1940 Packard™, as our assault vehicle. I even thought about how I could shoot it at targets inside the house on rainy days.

Even after proving to my parents that it was impossible for fat Santa with a sack of toys to get past the flue in our chimney, I always found a red and white stocking hung on the fireplace mantle on Christmas morning. It always had a tag—from Santa. It was filled with little things for school, like pencils, erasers, lots of candy, and a huge navel orange. Navel oranges were special back then, pricy at any food stores and hard to find. We didn't have big supermarkets back then like we have today with

56

food flown in from all over the world. Mendham only had a small general store down on West Main Street where you could shop for a limited number of essential items.

Since I no longer believed in Santa Claus, Mom would ask me for a wish list of what I wanted for Christmas. The cork gun was going at the top of the list. Back then, you only got one or two things that you really wanted for Christmas and the rest were clothes for school and church. Now that I was getting older and smarter than my parents were, I would outsmart them by writing just one thing on my list—a cork gun. This wouldn't give them a choice to buy something else.

The craziness of Christmas had passed; the family dinner, the present exchange, and most of the holiday food and sweets eaten. Preparations began for New Year's Eve.

It was New Year's Eve and my parent's tradition was to invite couples from the neighborhood over for cocktails and hors-d'oeuvres, dinner, evening munchies, and more cocktails. Dad had set up a table on our sunporch with all sorts of liquors, that he called spirits. I thought that was a perfect name for them since everyone's attitude and spirit seemed to change after consuming one or two glasses of the stuff.

My mom and the other wives drank what Mom called a 'ladies drink.' It was either wine or for the daring ones, a mixer with a tiny amount of spirits. There were two mixers that I was allowed to have, ginger ale and Coke™. I also was allowed to put one of those cherries with the long stems into my drink. If no one was watching, I would put plop in several!

My parent's New Year's Eve party was one extravagant event. Mom made what she called a standing rib roast with a decorative paper crown over the top of the ribs in a complete circle. The main entree was served with baked potatoes and vegetables. The vegetables were ones she had frozen from our home garden.

It was after the second round of initial cocktails when the spirits that were inside those bottles took effect.

The noise of the conversations and laughter had risen to a noisy and boisterous level. There were no other kids there for me to play with, so all I could do was sit on the floor by the fireplace and watch the adults get silly until dinner.

After dinner and dessert, Mom suggested that they all play cards, a game called Pinochle. At this point in time, the guys got the better end of the deal. Mom and all the wives had kitchen duty making numerous trips back and forth to the kitchen with all the leftover food and dirty dishes. And what did the guys do? Jabber and tell jokes. This was another time in my life that I was glad to be born a boy. Sometime later, Mom pulled out a deck of cards for a challenging evening of Pinochle and turned on *Lawrence Welk* on our little black and white TV.

This was the one night of the year I was allowed to stay up late—midnight. I enjoyed all the snacks my mother placed out for our guests, especially the celery stuffed with cream cheese and figs stuffed with peanut butter and sprinkled with sugar. I remember, laughing to myself watching the adults get sillier as the evening progressed that coincided with the consumption of spirits. No one ever got drunk or collapsed on the floor from the stuff as I had after drinking all that beer at our Fourth of July party.

They played cards in our dining room, everyone sitting around the large rectangular wooden table festively decorated for the holiday season. I sat in the living room in front of the crackling fireplace playing with one of my Christmas presents, not on my list. It was a building set of small ceramic bricks along with window and doorframes. The set included a small tube of glue to stick everything together. I wanted to build a barn, but kicked that idea out of my head—I never saw a barn made of red bricks. Then it hit me, build an experimental lab, like that guy Edison, the inventor.

Taking a break now and then, to let the glue harden a bit, I thought about all the experiments and things I would like to build in the New Year.

Maybe I'de build one of those Geiger counters in case the Russians bomb Washington. That would come in really handy for my pals and me.

I could hear the adults having lots of fun. They were laughing, kidding one another, and having a great time. There were moans as some had been dealt a bad hand and those staying silent waiting to display their good luck, and finally, someone would slap down their cards with a winning hand. Some years, they played with quarters. Being a very religious family my mother had to justify the use of money. Gambling was a no, no, something our family never did. To make it morally okay, she would always say it was to make the game interesting. And this was another year to keep the game interesting—playing with quarters. All the players had stacks of quarters in front of them.

Hans and his wife, Alice, one of the couples, were invited this year as always for the get-together. Hans was of German descent, a short guy with reddish hair and a wide mustache; he twisted and waxed each end to a point. He worked as a tool and die maker, where precision and accuracy were always required. Being precise was part of his personality, too, no matter what he did, including playing cards.

Shortly after the card game started, around nine o'clock, he complained to my dad about the noise of the cuckoo clock. It was unfortunate that my mother placed him at the table right under the clock that hung on the wall—real close and personal. He was concentrating on his hand of cards when the cuckoo bird came out and began doing his thing, nine times.

"Walt, can't you shut that damn clock off? I'm having one hell of a time concentrating!"

"Hans! Be polite, we're guests here." Alice, his wife, sharply set his manners straight.

Everyone stopped talking, stayed as quiet as a mouse, so as to not re-ignite Han's over the top anger. Conversations and cocktails soon continued, once again. An hour later when the cuckoo clock began striking ten o'clock, I could see the tension building up in Hans, displayed by the tapping of his closed fist on the table. When I went to get another glass of soda, I noticed that his eyes were really bloodshot, even bulging out a little bit. I didn't know if that was from staring at his cards, being mad at the clock, too much booze, or from all three of those combined.

However, the game took an interesting twist with him winning the next round when the clock struck eleven. His luck went south after that when I noticed his stacks of quarters almost completely gone. Shortly before midnight, he started to complain again to his wife.

"It's that damn clock! I'm having one hell of a time memorizing the cards that are being played. Walt, if you don't stop that damn cuckoo clock, I will!" he shouted.

He slammed his fist on the table. Alice looked at him and said, "Go take a walk, Hans."

As Hans got up from the table and walked into the living room where I was, the cuckoo clock went crazy starting its midnight, New Year's Eve cuckooing. Everyone hugged, kissed, wished all a happy new year; everyone but Hans. I was lying next to the Christmas tree, almost asleep, when I saw his big hand reach for the cork gun that was next to me.

What's he going to do with my gun? I watched him walk with determination back into the dining room, take aim, and fire a shot at the cuckoo clock. *He's also precise with a gun,* I thought, as I saw the bird fall off his little perch dropping to the floor with a dull thud. The kissing stopped immediately! The room went into complete silence with the bird stone dead laying on the floor and everyone staring at it as the clock finished its midnight strike, bird less.

Looking really pissed, Dad looked Hans in the eye and asked, "What did you do that for? That's an expensive Black Forest Clock™."

Hans returned the gaze and retorted, "Not anymore."

Chapter 6

Granddaddy

Mendham Borough, NJ 1951

In my hometown of Mendham, wildlife was abundant, a paradise for kids, like myself, to witness growing up. Box turtles were one of our favorite things to catch. They were harmless and easy to capture. As a turtle saw the danger, its head would disappear inside its shell and a protective flap would close to keep out the predator—us, a dog, or anything else. We liked to bring them inside our homes as pets, placing them securely into a cardboard box. The poor turtle made endless circles trying to get out. It also stood on its back legs and reached up with its front ones trying to reach the top of the box. Feeling guilty, we would run outside to get grass and earthworms for them to eat. Unfortunately, the grass only wilted and worms rotted away sometime later, stinking up a bedroom or some other place in the home.

Sometimes, they were brought to school for 'show and tell,' usually with a new given name. A few days after the capture, our parents would say, "It's going to die, take it outside and let it go." Begrudgingly, feeling sorry for the poor turtle, we returned it to the backyard.

Chipmunks were abundant, too. They were really cute, so cute that we often wanted them as pets, as well. Fortunately, they were faster than us, but not the family cat. Most of the time they were dead by the time we'd catch the cat. Sometimes, it would still be alive or seriously injured with a broken back and in great pain. Dad would have to put it out of its misery.

Our cat, Kemglo, got lucky one Saturday morning and caught one. I happened to be outside at the time and rescued the poor chipmunk.

It appeared to have perished as I removed it from Kemglow's mouth and sadly cradled it in my hands and brought it inside the house to show my parents. Dad and Mom were there in the sunroom reading the newspaper as John Gambling rambled away on WOR radio in the background. I brought it over to show Dad, holding it between his newspaper and his face to get his attention.

"Why are you bringing that dead animal into the house? It might have some disease," Dad said, with alarm.

Mom got up out of her chair to look at the little creature. "Aw, the poor little fellow."

She must have had some soothing healing power because the chipmunk opened its eyes, jumped out of my hands, and down on my father's lap to the floor, scaring the bejesus out of him. Soon, it was two adults and me chasing the poor thing all over the house until it ran under the stove.

"See what happens when you bring wild animals into the house?" Dad said, pissed-off in total disgust. He continued, "I'm going to get Kemglo."

"No way, Dad! I'll catch him."

Hours went by and Dad was getting impatient. It wasn't until late afternoon when I successfully threw a blanket over the little guy and released him safely outside—lesson learned.

Then there were the slithery things—snakes. Garter snakes were most prevalent, all over Mendham. Once in a while, a black snake would make an appearance. They were mostly found around farms that raised chickens. I noticed snakes early on when I saw them warming themselves on large rocks or wrapped around branches on low bushes, bathing in the warmth of the sun.

I would cautiously walk up to them to get a closer look. They would flick their forked tongues and stare at me with their beady eyes. On one occasion, I found one and ran into the house to tell Dad.

"Dad, I found a snake in the flower garden, do they bite?"

"No, not at all, they're good to have around the yard. They eat a lot of insects."

Over and over again, I would ask Dad the same question. "Do they bite?" He always came back with the same answer.

"No."

As I got a little older, I would approach one, ready to wrap my fingers around it, but chicken out at the last minute. Sometimes, it would simply slither off into the bushes.

Clean-up day in Mendham happened once or twice a year, a time for residents to throw out all their old junk. For us, it was a treasure trove, a source of material to build something with. There would be non-working radios, bicycles or anything else you could imagine sitting on the curb. On this particular clean-up day, there was a rectangular fish tank, perhaps one that leaked. The wheels in my brain didn't have to turn too many times to figure out a use for it—a reptile or snake tank! I took it home.

When I got home, I got a pail of hot soapy water and a brush from inside the house and cleaned the tank until it was spotless. After it dried in the sun, I brought it into my bedroom awaiting my first creature to capture.

A few weeks later I spotted the biggest garter snake I'd ever seen. It must have been the granddaddy of all the Mendham snakes. I still, didn't quite believe my father's words of wisdom, so I got a cardboard box with flaps to collect it. *I'm going to call him Granddaddy.*

With the box by my feet, I got up really close and clapped my hands to scare him. He dropped down from the bush to the ground, slithering in that infamous 'S' pattern. Granddaddy sort of made me dizzy, as I chased after him with my box. I got ahead of him and slammed the box on its side and he went right into it. With the flaps closed, I carried him into the house and dropped him into the glass tank.

He wasn't happy, trying to find a way out. I quickly placed a piece of perforated cardboard over the top to keep him safely inside.

I had no idea what garter snakes ate and needed to look it up in the library the next day. As bedtime approached, nine on Little Ben, my clock, it was time to hit the sack. I checked on Granddaddy, and he was ready to go to sleep, too, curled up in a perfect circle.

I didn't sleep too well, I kept on having reoccurring nightmares about snakes. The worst one, the one that woke me up, was about a huge snake, big enough to swallow me. He was angry with me for capturing his son. He chased me across the backyard and into the haunted red barn, up the stairs to the hayloft over by the sliding door. I had two choices, slide the door open and jump down two stories or get eaten by the snake—I took the first option and woke up just before hitting the ground.

Amazed that I was still alive, I tried to get back to sleep—it took me forever. Morning arrived, and I opened my eyes, and looked over at my glass tank—no snake! Granddaddy was gone!

The cardboard cover had been pushed aside and Granddaddy had gained his freedom somewhere in the warm house. I began to search my room, under the bed, under my blankets; he was nowhere to be found. My closet door was closed, so he couldn't be there. My mom and dad were still asleep. Before they got up, I searched every room, but their bedroom. *What if he slithered into their room and found a good hiding place? Maybe it was up one leg of dad's trousers that he always folded over on his chair.*

Dad got up before Mom. From the hallway, I could hear him stirring around getting dressed. I held my breath. When he walked out of their room, I exhaled in relief that he hadn't had a snake encounter so early in the morning—a snake staring him in the face. He saw me standing there in the hall, doing nothing. "What are you up to?"

I shuffled my feet, smiled and said, "Nothing, Dad."

64

"I know you're up to something—you've got that familiar guilty look."

"Just waiting for you to wake up, Dad, for you to make your famous flapjacks."

"That sounds good for a Sunday morning," he replied, heading for the kitchen, whistling a happy tune.

He had no idea how his happy day was about to be ruined! Dad headed for the kitchen, with me following him a few paces behind until I did a sneaky 'U'y for my bedroom to get my flashlight and check out their bedroom for Granddaddy. They had two beds, so I checked under the sheet, blanket, and under his bed—no Granddaddy. Mom was snoring away, deep in sleep. I turned on the flashlight to check under her bed and the other pieces of furniture—he wasn't there either.

Days went by and Granddaddy hadn't shown up. This was day four, Mom's cleaning day; she came into my room with her vacuum cleaner. As she walked in, she stared at my empty tank.

"What happened to the snake? I hope you let it loose outside."

I paused to think about how to answer her question, I didn't want to lie, but I remembered someone telling me a 'white lie' was okay. So I avoided eye contact, said in a soft voice, "Yeah, loose, Mom."

Mom started the vacuum with the wide attachment over the carpeting. After completing the floor, she removed the attachment and used the end of the vacuum hose to do all around the molding and under the furniture. I hoped that I hadn't missed finding the snake, because if I had, Granddaddy would be in for a ride of his life—haha!

I just knew in my head either Dad or Mom would come across him sooner or later. I hoped that this would not turn out to be the day. Dad had worked most of the day planting our vegetable garden. I heard him say to Mom, "I'm going to get cleaned up and take a shower."

I forgot to check the shower. I ran for the shower and opened the shower curtain—he wasn't there either, thank God.

I had hoped that Granddaddy found his way outside. It was after Dad had finished his evening cocktail and was seated at the kitchen table for dinner, that I found out I was dead wrong. There he was, wrapped around the long coiled telephone wire on the wall phone (Mom had the telephone company put the long wire on so she could talk and cook at the same time). His beady eyes stared at me as he stuck his tongue out several times.

We began dinner. With each forkful, I made sure he stayed in his special spot. *He must be hungry, probably waiting for some leftovers.* Luckily, no one called on the phone and neither parent needed to make a call or noticed him hanging there.

After dinner, Mom asked, "Anyone for dessert?"

"None for me, Mom."

"Me either," Dad said, looking really tired.

To keep an eye on him, I volunteered to help Mom with the dishes.

"Well, that's so nice of you to help. Why don't you dry?"

When we finished, Mom headed into the other room to join Dad. After the coast was clear, I carefully grabbed Granddaddy behind his head with my right hand and unwrapped him with my other hand from the cord. I got to the back door and needed to turn the doorknob. So, I let go of his body as I held him behind his head. In a second, he was wrapped around my wrist, scaring the wits out of me. Outside, I unwrapped him from my wrist and tried to let him go, but he didn't let go of me. He bit down in anger on my index finger and wrapped himself around my wrist and held on. Frightened out of my mind. I tried to shake him off, but he held on. I yelled, at the top of lungs, "Help! Help! Dad, help me!"

Dad, hearing all the screaming, got out of his comfortable chair and ran outside to where I was standing.

"Dad! Get this evil snake off me!"

"Stop waving your hands all over the place so I can remove it."

"He's hurting me, Dad!"

Dad got him off and threw him on the ground. The snake took off across the grass for the bushes.

"Dad! Dad! Look at my finger, it's bleeding! Look at all the blood! You told me garter snakes don't bite!"

"I guess I was wrong, but what were you doing picking up a garter snake?" he asked.

"I don't want to talk about it, Dad."

Chapter 7

Saturday Movie Matinees: Bring a Helmet

Mendham Borough, NJ 1951

Mendham parents, including mine, sometimes out of kindness and sometimes out of desperation would say on a rainy Saturday, "How about going to the movies?" This was a special treat since money was tight and most families didn't go to the movies that often in the fifties. Since Mendham didn't have a movie theater, it meant going to one of the two theaters in Morristown; the Park Theater located on the square or the Community Theater on South Street.

Most families back then got a daily newspaper. The most popular was *The Morristown Daily Record* because it covered local news stories. The paper included an entertainment section listing all the current movies showing in the area theaters. The performances on the weekend afternoons were called matinees, tailored to entertain children.

Since my mom had given up driving, my dad drove us to Morristown. Dad would let me invite one or two friends to go with me to the matinee. He would set down some basic rules, like staying inside the theater until he came to pick us up. He also made sure we all had enough money for our tickets and a little extra, just in case.

It was a Friday evening and the weather forecast was for rain throughout the entire weekend—a real soaker. Dad knocked on my door holding the newspaper's entertainment section. I opened the door to see what he wanted.

"It's going to be a rainy weekend. Would you like to invite some friends to go to the movies tomorrow afternoon?" he asked.

"Yippy! That would be fun Dad. How many friends may I invite?"

"One or two would be fine. Here's a list of what's playing in Morristown."

I ran out of my room for the kitchen with the paper trailing behind me like a paper kite in the breeze. I lifted the telephone off the kitchen wall, heard the click, then waited for the operator to pick-up.

The operator asked, "What party, please?"

"The De Groot residence, please."

A few moments later, she said, "Your party is connected."

"This is Mrs. De Groot."

"May I speak to Jimmy?"

"Sure, hold on, I'll get him. Jimmy! It's Greg on the phone."

"Hi, Buddy—what's cooking?" Jimmy asked.

"Want to go to the movies tomorrow?"

"Yeah!" he said.

I read-off what was playing and we decided to see *Superman and the Mole Men* playing at The Park Theater in Morristown. Dad would not be happy, not because of the film we chose, but the theater that it was playing at. He always encouraged me to go to the Community Theater—it was safer.

The Community Theater (now the Mayo) was a first-class movie theater establishment. The building was classy in its ornate architecture structure with fancy columns, majestic dome, and comfortable seating. The ushers were first-class, too. They dressed very formally in their meticulously clean maroon and white uniforms with smart vests decorated with shiny brass buttons up the front. They stood straight, just like military men, took your ticket and some offered to usher you down the aisle, but we always declined.

70

They had another responsibility, too—disciplinarians. They were really good at that job. My friends and I knew that they had been professionally trained by their efficiency on pulling a problem kid out of the theater in a split second. They meant business—a tap on the shoulder and you were out the door in a flash. My buddies and I were convinced they all must have been trained by our school principal, Mr. Latterlee.

The snack bar was something else at the Community. The second you walked through the front door, you smelled the aroma of freshly prepared buttery popcorn. It sort of clobbered you in the face. Giant-sized candy bars and boxes of Raisenits™, Good & Plenty™, Sno-Caps™, and several others were neatly lined up behind the glass counter. Then there was the soda fountain service. Everything was expensive. Maybe if we were lucky, our parents gave us money to buy a small soda and candy bar.

You weren't supposed to bring snacks from home into the Community Theater. But we, the Mendham kids, broke that rule every time. It wasn't our fault, it was our parents. They suggested that we bring our snacks because we had to be thrifty—money was tight. It made us feel like young criminals with snacks stuffed everywhere possible. During the winter months, that was easy. We just stuffed the glass soda bottle and snacks under our coats and hoped that they stayed in place.

During the warmer weather, when we wore shorts and a T-shirt, we had to be creative. Pockets didn't hold much, especially for us growing boys. So we stuffed the snacks under our undershirts. Sometimes a kid would stuff so many snacks and drinks that he took on a Santa Claus appearance with a big gut. The maroon usher would stop him and tell him to dump the stuff in the waste container. It was embarrassing when a snack of potato chips you stuffed under the front of your T-shirt, mysteriously worked its way to the back. Sometimes you realized that too late when you sat back in your seat and heard the chips crunch. You had to just sit there with the chips sort of digging into your back until the lights dimmed and the movie ushers disappeared.

Before the feature film began, they featured newsreels, which were historical short films. Often, they were past military battles from WWII. As boys, we really loved watching these battles. After our history lesson, they ran cartoons on the silver screen. Most of the time we enjoyed watching these more than the main attraction. The theater exploded with kids laughter as Woody Woodpecker and Bugs Bunny popped-up on the screen. We always enjoyed going to the Community Theater and would talk about our experience all the way back to Mendham after the show.

The Park Theater was an old and dated theater after many years of entertaining patrons. The theater did not have the best reputation, and was especially notorious for their lack of discipline, especially when it was an all kids audience on a weekend. To compete against the other theater, they often had a lower ticket price. The first thing you noticed when you put your foot in the door was its appearance. No matter where you looked it appeared old and dirty, but as kids, we didn't care, we were there to see the movie. Another thing we noticed as we came through the door was the buttered popcorn had a sort of an off aroma. Perhaps the snack bar reheated what was not sold the night before. The fountain sodas didn't fizz out of the nozzle no matter which lever the guy pulled; the drinks sometimes came out flat without carbonation. We just walked right by the snack area, since we brought our own snacks and lined-up for the movie.

On Saturday as I finished my lunch, I said to my dad, "We're going to see *Superman and the Mole.*"

"That sounds like a good movie. What time does it start?"

"Two."

"I'll drop you and your friends off at the Community at quarter-to-two."

"It's playing at the Park, Dad."

With a cringed expression Dad said, "I don't want you to go there. Pick another movie—at the Community."

"No, Dad! We want to see *Superman*!"

"A lot of hoodlums hang out at the Park. I don't feel comfortable with you going there."

"There are three of us, Jimmy, Will, and me. We can take care of ourselves."

"That's what I'm afraid of, too. You kids getting into a rumble with those troublemakers."

Somehow I convinced my dad that everything would be all right. Jimmy and Will arrived at the house and we jumped into Dad's Plymouth™ sedan for the trip to Morristown.

"I bet you guys are really looking forward to seeing *Superman*."

"We are, Mr. Smith," Will said, wearing a big smile.

"Thank you for inviting us to go with Greg," Jimmy said with appreciation.

"I want you guys to be careful there at the Park. There are some bad kids that go there."

"We'll be fine, Dad."

Dad parked the car and gave us each some bills and we jumped out, slammed the doors closed, and ran to the theater entrance before he changed his mind on letting us go there. We knew he had more words of wisdom to tell us, but we wanted to be spared the drama. We each handed the guy behind the window the bills for our tickets and headed inside the theater.

Jimmy and I had forgotten to go before leaving Mendham and we needed to use the men's room, really badly, before the show. We walked in and stopped in our tracks when we saw the flooded floor—it was gross!

"You know what they need to do Gregsy?" Jimmy said. "They need to put big gun targets on each one of the urinals. Maybe the kids would aim better."

We walked on our tiptoes to where we needed to be. Afterward, we looked at the filthy sinks and water faucet handles, no soap or paper towels, and decided our hands would be healthier if we didn't clean-up and headed for the exit.

This was my fourth time at the Park. After surviving the bathroom experience we waited in line and wondered why so many kids had paper straws without cups of soda to put them in. Will, Jimmy, and I reached the guy collecting tickets. We each handed him our ticket. He briefly inspected each one and dumped them into a green metal disposal stand and let us through.

We walked down the aisle to a row of seats near the screen. Will went in first, kicking the empty paper soda cups and popcorn containers out of the way, down under the next row of seats. Jimmy and I followed him in and we all sat down.

This theater liked to keep the lights low, probably to hide the filthy condition of the seats—the collected grime over many years. I made the mistake of touching the underside of my seat cushion. There must have been ten years of accumulated chewing gum there.

We goofed around as the theater filled with kids without parents in tow. Later, the lights dimmed to complete darkness as a newsreel began—WWII Navy engagement with a fighter squadron of Japanese Zeroes. The machine guns aboard the Destroyer Aylwin were firing at the enemy aircraft with the tracers lighting up the screen. I was really into it, holding onto the seat in front of me like it was a machine gun aboard the Aylwin.

"There's one coming to you at two o'clock!" I yelled.

Then I got clobbered with a round that hit me in the back of my neck. It stung like hell! I elbowed Jimmy and whispered in his ear, "I just got shot."

74

"You're nuts! Your imagination is running away with you," he said, as he turned back to watch the action.

I sat back in my seat rubbing my wound that felt wet and sloppy. Was it blood? I go back into the battle and took a second hit, this time in the back of the head. "Jimmy, I just got nailed again, this time in my head."

Jimmy turned towards me and said, "You're absolutely nuts, you know that?" when he brought his hand to his face and shouted, "Ow! I just got shot, too! In the cheek!"

"See, smarty, I told you I got shot twice."

"You're right Gregsy, those kids with the straws are sitting behind us shooting spitballs," Jimmy said with alarm. "Will, we're getting bombarded with spitballs, we're changing our seats."

"Okay. No one got me yet," Will said, as he took a sloppy hit in the forehead.

We stumbled out of our seats in the dark and moved to a row of empty seats near the back. The newsreel finished and Woody Woodpecker came on the screen. We laughed at Woody Woodpecker's antics, which put us all in a better mood.

Superman and the Mole, the feature film, started, and the three of us were glued to the screen enjoying it. Before we knew it, the movie ended and the lights came on. We all got up to leave when I missed seeing the big wad of sticky gum on the floor in front of me and stepped right on it. Every time my left foot touched the floor, it felt as if it had been glued to it. I came out of the theater limping.

"Did you take a hit in the leg, too?" Jimmy shouted as I followed him and Will to the exit. "There's your dad, you better move a little faster!"

I had a hard time keeping up with the guys. I looked up and saw my dad quizzically staring at me, hobbling behind my friends.

"What in God's name happened to your leg?" he asked with concern.

Before I could answer, Jimmy yelled, "He took two hits in a naval battle aboard the Aylwin!"

I said, with a snicker, "Stepped on a big wad of gum."

"Be sure to take your sticky shoe off before you sit in my car," Dad commanded like a naval officer.

"Aye, aye sir," I replied.

On the way home, Jimmy made the mistake of telling my dad about the spitball episode.

"That's the last time you go to the Park. I knew there'd be trouble—I just knew it."

As my dad drove us home, I thought of how much fun we'd had, as I plucked a few more spitballs out of my hair. I couldn't wait to go back, maybe with a straw!

Chapter 8

Bankrupt at Ten

Because of Twenty-four Little Peckers

Mendham Borough, NJ 1952

It happened Saturday morning, the day before Easter, when I was ten years old. My dad asked if I would like to take a ride over to GF Hill in Peapack. He knew what the answer would be, even before he asked me.

"Are you kidding? My favorite place!" I zoomed out the door to the red barn at the back of the property where Dad garaged his car. Arriving before Dad, I slid open the large garage door and waited for his arrival.

"May I go see the new Farmall™ tractors, Dad?"

"Sure! Under one condition," Dad said, as we got into the car.

"What's that, Dad?"

"That you don't pester the salesman to start one."

"Okay," I said with my fingers and legs crossed, with hope to do just that.

We headed out the long gravel driveway for Main Street on our way to Peapack, about twenty minutes away. Dad needed to get some cabinet hinges for the kitchen renovation project he was working on.

Arriving at the little country town, Dad parked the car and we entered the old hardware store. This was the kind of building when you walked on the floor, you heard each floorboard complain with a loud creak.

I loved to come here. They had all sorts of electrical stuff, especially those large six-volt lantern batteries that could power my experiments. Too bad I couldn't afford to buy one. My favorite things in the store were on display—replica Farmall™ tractor models and farm accessories. They kept these on a shelf, high on the wall, away from the many little anxious hands that tried to reach them. When I was younger, I started collecting them, one by one. I would play with them on the floor pretending to be a farmer. What made them special was that each one worked like the real machines.

It would take me several months to buy one. Each Friday my dad handed me a handful of pennies that accumulated on his chest of drawers. When I collected fifty, I stuffed them into a paper tube to join the others that I had saved. When I collected eight tubes, I had enough to buy a model.

Dad bought his hinges and said, "Ready to go down and check out the tractors?"

"Yup! Meet you down there," I said, as I shot out of the hardware store for the tractor showroom.

GF Hill had a brand-new showroom several hundred feet down the hill from their hardware store. Running as fast as I could, I sailed through the air with every step. I reached the showroom door in record time.

I flung open the door to see the large Farmall™ tractor parked in front of me. The aroma of the new rubber tires and fresh red paint entered my nose as I headed to touch the huge machine. This model was much bigger than ours, it towered above me, and most certainly above my dad too. It was a machine to use on a large farm.

Peeking around the tractor, I saw Mr. Harrison, the tractor salesman. He was sitting at his desk shuffling papers. Leonard had sold us our tractor and snowplow attachment. I think that's why he allowed me to play with the tractors. He lifted his eyes and caught me peeking around the machine at him. He quickly got out of his chair and headed over to me.

"Come to play with the tractors, Greg?"

"You bet!"

"I'm going to pull the key out to be on the safe side. Where's your dad?"

"On his way over."

The telephone rang on Mr. Harrison's desk. "I've got to get that—have fun with the tractor!"

My hands explored the heavy machine, the engine, radiator, and steering mechanism. Dad walked in just as I was checking out the front tires. Leonard finished his call and got up from his desk when he saw my Dad.

"Hi, Walt! Ready to upgrade yours for one of these?" Leonard said, as he pointed to the tractor at the center of the showroom floor.

"Yeah, Dad! That's a great idea!"

"That's all I need to do! Jan still hasn't forgiven me for blowing my Christmas bonus on that Model A Farmall™ you sold me two years ago."

"It wasn't the tractor, Walt. It was the two Merc's that got delivered, too. Our delivery guys really enjoy retelling that story. Telling how Lotz Lincoln-Mercury arrived with two Merc's and our guys with the tractor; all at the same time with your wife's arms going as fast as an airplane propeller, telling everyone, 'They're not ours! They're not ours!'" Leonard said, then added. "She nearly fainted when both delivery men asked, 'Is this the Walter Smith residence?'"

"Yeah, she took it hard. She pinches pennies to put something in the bank each month for a rainy day."

"You should have warned her, Walt. Look at your son over there. Did you ever see a kid so interested in tractors? He might end up being a farmer someday, just so he could drive them. Let me go over and help him get up on the seat."

I saw my Dad and Leonard walking towards me laughing about something.

"Would you like to sit on the seat?" Mr. Harrison asked.

"Yeah! How do I get up there? You need to have legs like a giant to climb up!"

"Here, climb up on the drawbar first, hold my hand so you can climb up to the seat."

I sat high up on the seat and squeezed my fingers around the wheel. I even turned the steering wheel a little bit, watching the tires move on the shiny tile floor. It felt like I died and went to kid heaven. *I'll have to remember to ask Pastor Philips, at church, if there are tractors in heaven.*

I pretended to be a farmer plowing his cornfield. I let out the clutch, hit the brake a few times and made a couple of turns. This was make-believe at its greatest!

"Want to buy it for him?" Leonard asked, wearing a big salesman's smile.

"Don't put any ideas in his head."

"I'll bet he can't wait to drive the Model A."

As they shot the breeze, I continued with my fantasy. It almost sounded like a farm with a zillion peeps coming from the back of the showroom.

"Mr. Harrison, what's making all those peeping sounds?"

"Baby chicks. Want to see them?"

"Later, after I spend some more time up here."

About twenty minutes later, Dad said to me, "We've got to get back so I can work on the kitchen project."

Dad helped me down to the drawbar and I jumped to the floor.

"Would you like a baby chick to take home for Easter? We're giving them away."

I followed Mr. Harrison over to the large cardboard container about a foot high with several red heating lamps glowing keeping the chicks warm. Inside were dozens of baby chicks, some red and others white. "Could I have one, Dad? Please! I'll take good care of it."

"Sure. We're going to have to buy a bag of chipped corn to feed it."

"How would you like two dozen? I've got to get rid of these things, hopefully before Easter."

"Sure, Mr. Harrison!" I shouted with excitement.

"May I have twelve red and twelve white ones?"

"Sure thing, let me get a box for you to take them home in. You'll need a roll of chicken wire along with that bag of feed."

"Leonard, you're a good salesman. You didn't sell me a bigger tractor, but you ended up selling me a roll of wire and a bag of cracked corn."

We loaded the wire and the food in the back of Dad's station wagon. I jumped in the front seat with my box of peeping chicks on my lap.

"Aren't they cute, Dad? I'm going to find names for each one. May I keep them in my bedroom?"

"Absolutely not."

"Please!"

"They have to be kept in the barn where they'll be safe from predators, like foxes and raccoons. We'll cordon off an area and place some straw so that they can cuddle up to stay warm."

"But they would be safer in my room Dad!"

"That's not going to happen," Dad quickly responded.

We got that done and set the food and water containers inside their area for them. They never stopped peeping from the time we got them. When I dropped their food in the saucer, they went crazy! They must have been hungry, as they climbed over one another to get at the food.

Dad said, "That should do it."

"You forgot one thing, Dad."

"What's that?"

"Who's going to protect them from the ghost?"

"I'm sorry I ever told you about that legend."

"It's no legend, Dad! That beastly ghost chased Al, Sam and me out of the barn one midnight!"

"I'm sure they'll be fine."

"There's twenty-four now. I better take a headcount tomorrow—got to make sure that ghost didn't have one or two for a midnight snack!"

****

On Sunday morning, while Dad was making flapjacks for breakfast, I ran out to the barn to check on the chicks. I slid the door all the way open. I wanted to get as much light inside to keep whatever loomed in there to stay hidden—ghosts don't like daylight. Did you ever try to count two dozen crazy chicks? It wasn't easy!

I got back to the house looking forward to breakfast. Dad had a stack ready for me.

"Twenty-four?"

"Yup! I guess the ghost wasn't hungry at all last night!"

"Did you feed them?"

"Yeah, I did. They ate every morsel we left for them yesterday."

The chicks grew fast, and they outgrew their temporary cardboard container. Ones that looked a little different, it was easy to come up with names for, which I did. Three weeks later, they needed to be placed outside with access to shelter. We rolled out the chicken wire and made a run for them attaching it to the barn. These things were no longer cute little chicks, but ugly little chickens with a red growth on top of their heads. I called them a bunch of peckers because they ate continuously all day long—peck, peck, peck.

****

Sunday evening we were sitting peacefully around the dinner table enjoying our dinner when Mom inquired about my chickens.

"How are your chickens doing? Any eggs yet?"

"Are you kidding? They eat 24-hours a day and haven't plopped one egg out yet. They're all just a bunch of little peckers!"

Mom slammed her hand down hard on the table and yelled, "If I ever hear you use that word again, it's the Ivory soap™™ punishment!"

"What's wrong with saying a bunch of little peckers?"

"It's a nasty word!"

****

At two months old, these little monsters were eating machines. They ate so much that my loot was disappearing fast buying bags of feed. I had gone through all my saved birthday money and Christmas money. The only money I had left were a few tubes of pennies saved for another model tractor.

Dad felt sorry for me, seeing me so depressed, so he went out and bought a bag of feed for the flock. That bag would last for a week, maybe two, if I put the peckers on a diet.

It got to the point that I hated these things. I even prayed that the ghost would get hungry and eat every single one of them. It was a lose, lose situation. They were no longer cute to pet and they were too young to lay eggs. Just a bunch of ugly chickens, good for only one thing—pecking!

Ten days later the food was nearly gone and I was dead broke. I had to tell Dad I only had enough food for another day and I no longer wanted them. We were having dinner when I popped the question. "Dad, do you think we can take these chickens back to Mr. Harrison?"

"I'm afraid not. Has the novelty of playing farmer worn off?"

"Are you kidding? I'm bankrupt! I don't have a penny to my name. What am I going to do?"

"I'll call my friend, Mr. Lowe, the sheep farmer, here in town. He'll take them. He can't resist a bargain, especially when it's a free one."

****

Several months later, after the chickens were gone, the front doorbell rang. Mom and I ran to see who was ringing our bell. It was Mr. Lowe the farmer, with two dead, de-feathered ugly chickens, one hanging from each hand.

I knew they were mine because I recognized their little heads and their foul smell. "What have you done to my chickens, Mr. Lowe?"

In his gravelly voice, with a big cigar hanging from his mouth, puffing away, he said, "I broke their necks and pulled their feathers out so your mom can cook them up for a roast chicken dinner."

"That's a crazy thing to do, Mr. Lowe! If I knew you were going to murder Jane and Alice, I'd have never given them to you!" I screamed as I ran off with tears running from my eyes.

"Thank you, John. We'll enjoy the chickens," Mom said.

It was about six in the afternoon when Mom called me for dinner. My Aunt Mildred and Uncle George came to visit us that afternoon and my mother invited them to stay for dinner. They were at the table when I arrived.

"Hi, Aunt Mildred and Uncle George," I said as I gave them both a hug and sat down at my place. Mom came in from the kitchen with a large meat platter with Jane and Alice next to one another and placed the platter next to Dad to carve up.

Dad said grace, "Dear Lord, thank you for this bountiful meal we are about to receive—Amen."

And I continued, "Please forgive me Jane and Alice for giving you to that awful farmer, Mr. Lowe—Amen.

I watched, as Dad plunged the cutting fork into the first bird and began to cut. She was my baby, the chick I fed and cared for over many weeks. Upset, I asked to be excused and headed for my bedroom.

Chapter 9

The Tug That Won the Game

Mendham Borough, NJ 1949-1952

It was 8:20 p.m. when Rudy Dugan raised his hand to make a well-prepared statement during a heated town council meeting at the Phoenix House. This was a special meeting, open for public comment, on building a community pool. In attendance were numerous people, packed in like sardines, for this evening's agenda. Rudy sat with a number of residents who opposed the pool project. Some feared a steep increase in property taxes; others were concerned with noise—kids screaming all day.

"The chair recognizes Mr. Dugan to speak," Chairman Roberts said, in a loud voice over the din in the crowded room.

Rudy Dugan stood up. He moved through those that were seated, bumping into many knees and shuffling through others that stood, to get to the floor microphone in front of the council, when the audio system suddenly let out a squeal. Someone in the audience shouted, "Rudy you're even making the microphone nervous on what you've got to say tonight!" The tension broke as everyone laughed, except Rudy.

"The gavel pounded hard on the table, with Roberts screaming, **"Order! Order!"**

Dugan looked back at his supporters and then adjusted the mic stand. He glanced briefly at his cheat sheet, an index card, making sure to hit on every point. Some heated attendees shifted in their seats and let out dissenting boos. Over the previous months, Rudy had written several editorials that were published in the local *Mendham Gazette* newspaper, criticizing the project from every possible aspect. He and his group of followers had an ax to grind—they always did.

"Mr. Chairman, Rudy Dugan, Mountain Avenue," he said, as his words echoed loudly in the room.

Several more boos broke out and one person yelled, "We've heard it all Rudy—sit down!"

"Order! Order!" shouted Roberts, after pounding his gavel several times.

With his hands clenched, he said loudly, "I strongly object to this ridiculous project!"

He was ready to continue when he heard the noise of children building up until it reached the room. He turned around and was dumbstruck to see a huge number of kids squeezing into chambers and all shouting in unison, "We need a pool! We need a pool! We need a pool!...."

The kids filled the open space in front of all the council members, as they continued with their chant. The reporter for the local newspaper inserted a flashbulb in his camera and stood on his chair to capture the action. He clicked the shutter knowing he had his lead story for next week's newspaper.

The chairperson saw enough, slammed his gavel down several times and shouted, "Officer, remove the children!" The mayor looked at the borough's police officer and motioned with his hand affirming Roberts' instruction as the kids chanted even louder; Not Fair! Not Fair! We want a pool!

Eric, a kid that had a mind of his own, sort of a smart alec, screamed at the top of his lungs, "We need a pool! You need a pool! Everyone needs a pool!" He was the last to leave, as the officer personally escorted him out of the meeting.

After the kids were removed, Rudy gave his well-prepared statement. A few other residents followed him with theirs. As the clock pointed to nine-thirty, Roberts closed the public comment part of the agenda and moved onto the next, to vote on the proposal. One by one, every council member answered with an aye to pass it.

Roberts announced, "Proposal so approved. Let it be recorded that it was unanimous."

An outburst of clapping immediately broke out from residents with young families, in favor of the pool.

Rudy and his neighbors marched out with disappointment written all over their red faces that were engorged with angry blood. He said to his supporters that surrounded him, "Now I'm going to have to sell my damn house!"

****

With town officials releasing $5,000 in funding, the project got started. Mayor Bowers appointed Cyril Birch to head up the project. He was known as a person that could get things done and recently completed a ball field project. To start the pool project planning a civil engineer would be needed. Cyril knew just the person, C.V. Guerin. The local engineer offered to donate his professional services.

Mountain Valley Pool was constructed on the site of Hoffman Pond located on the four and a half acres off of Mountain Avenue after it was acquired from two private owners, Peter Clement, and Pitney Farms.

The start date arrived and many Mendham residents volunteered to work building the pool. They worked relentlessly for the good of the community. C.V. Guerin, a local engineer, donated his time to do all the civil engineering. John Parillo, a mason, provided all the masonry work and poured a new dam at no charge to the town.

Other residents, donated shrubs, and grass seed to beautify the grounds. Many of the town's fathers had worked with picks and shovels to provide all the required digging and manual labor. Back in the late 40's backhoes were not around. They would have made the project a lot easier and eliminated the many-blistered hands of the men swinging a pick and digging with a shovel.

Upon completion, Mendham Borough requested the required state inspection and approval to open Mountain Valley Pool. Unfortunately, for the kids, the first summer the pool didn't open because of the delayed inspection. However, when wintertime arrived and the ice froze to a sufficient thickness, the facility opened for ice-skating. Wooden platforms were fabricated to place on the ice for skaters to change into and out of their skates.

Mountain Valley Pool (Courtesy Richard Willis)

The following summer the swimming facility opened. My mother and I joined, paying a total of four dollars for our membership, a real bargain. After handing over the fee, we got our Mt. Valley tags and were ready to use the pool on opening day.

****

On a scorching Friday morning, I sat in the kitchen in front of an oscillating fan trying to get cool. It was the third day of an awful heat wave. It felt wonderful as the breeze swept back and forth over my face, evaporating my sweat. The telephone rang and Mom answered it.

"Hi, Joan!" She paused for a few moments and said, "That would be wonderful," and hung up.

"They just opened the town's pool. Do you want to check it out? Mrs. Johnson offered to take us there in her new car. She'll be here in a half-hour, around ten."

"Don't have to ask me twice," I said, as I ran off to my bedroom to change into my bathing suit.

"I'll pack a lunch along with soda and snacks so we can stay there most of the day," Mom said.

Thirty minutes later, I was waiting with my towel on our front porch when Mrs. Johnson's blue Buick Roadmaster™ went around the circular driveway and stopped at our front porch. She was a chemistry teacher and off for the summer. My mother ran out the front door, out of breath, with our lunch basket and her stuff. I slid in the back on the gray velour seats and sat next to Jack.

He was a year younger than me, going into third grade in the fall. Mom put the things she was carrying next to me on the seat and closed the door. She got into the front seat with Mrs. Johnson and jabbered with her for the two-mile ride to the pool. We made a right turn into the parking lot and I saw the biggest pool I had ever seen—it looked more like a lake than a swimming pool.

"Jack! Have you ever seen such a monster pool? It even has a small island with a few trees!" I said.

"It looks like a lake!" he exclaimed.

"I thought the same thing."

Everyone got out of the car. As I slid off my seat, I looked down at my bare feet and the sharp gravel and said, "Mom, I forgot my sneakers."

"Well, you're too heavy, I can't carry you."

"I took a step and it felt like I stepped on red hot razor blades. **OW!**" I screamed.

"Use your towel and mine to reach the grass," Mom said, as she handed me her towel.

That was the first time I walked on a towel sidewalk!

I got to the grass where the others had been patiently waiting for me, as I flip-flopped the two towels to reach the grass.

"Next time wear your sneakers," Mom said, not looking any too happy.

The four of us headed for the wooden bridge. It spanned the stream that fed water into Mountain Valley Pool. My eyes were focused on the rowboat out in the center of the pool. The guy was dumping what looked like blue stones into the lake.

"Look at that guy dumping rocks in the pool. What's he doing that for, they just built the pool and he's trying to fill it in?" I said.

"That's copper-sulfate to keep away weeds and algae," Mrs. Johnson said.

We got to the top of the bridge when Jack and I stopped and peeked over the railing looking for fish. Our mothers continued on their way to the sandy beach. We didn't see anything, except for a small turtle, sticking its head out of the water at us. Not seeing any fish, we ran towards the swimming area, while our mothers sat on their blankets, spread out on the sandy beach, having a conversation.

Reaching the water, Jack and I ran in, splashing water on each other with every step—it felt good and cooled us down. Further out in knee-deep water was a teenage lifeguard giving swimming lessons. She had her students all lined-up in front of her showing them how to move their arms in the water to swim. Jack and I stood in front of the group and watched. Neither of us knew how to swim.

She turned, saw us watching, and said, "Do you want to join us?"

"Sure!" we said and joined the other seven kids.

92

Mountain Valley Pool (Courtesy Richard Willis)

She instructed us to wade into shallower water, to practice kicking. We all did that without any problem. She had us move out further, where the water was deeper.

"Now, one at a time, try to swim to me. Some kids took two strokes and temporarily submerged like a submarine, going into panic mode with arms flying in every direction. One girl tried and sunk, too, coughing out water that she had swallowed. The instructor looked at me and said, "It's your turn."

"Okay! Here I come! Watch this!" Well, I ended up half-swimming to her. It was my last-minute decision to impress her. I used my hands, touching along the bottom, to scramble over the murky water and kicked like mad, pretending to swim, hoping she didn't notice. I was the only one that managed to reach her.

I stood up, looked up at her, squinting with the sun in my eyes and a big smile, and said, "I made it, aren't you proud of me?"

"Let's see you do it again, this time using your arms. Back you go," she said.

I tried what she taught us and sunk immediately, just like a rock. Moments later, my head popped out of the water, like the turtle we saw back at the bridge. She stood in front of me, making sure I didn't drown.

She said, "Just keep on practicing and you'll get it. I hope to see you at our next session tomorrow."

Jack must have chickened out with the swimming test; he was no longer with our group. He was over near the bridge, close to the water, looking at something. I headed his way, to see what he was up to. When I reached him, I asked, "What're you doing?"

"Trying to catch a frog, this place is full of frogs! Let's try to catch one!" Jack said.

"Well, you're talking to an expert frog catcher, watch how it's done, buddy." I got down on all fours and crept along in the tall grass, like a cat stalking its prey. It didn't take long before I spotted one, about three feet away. I moved in closer, first one hand and then the next, all the while staring at two eyes that stared right back at me. I got a little closer, when without warning; it escaped with one jump into the pool.

Jack broke out laughing and said, "Some expert frog catcher you are!"

After several more attempts to capture one, without success, Jack got bored and left me with the frogs, as he departed for the swimming area. Shortly after Jack left, I saw another frog higher up on the bank. I positioned myself between the pond and it, knowing what his escape plan would be. In one quick pounce, I had the slimy thing tightly in my hands. I got up, ran over to where Jack was and showed him my prized frog.

"Jack! See, I caught one! Told you I was an expert catcher, take a look."

"He's a cute little fella. What are you going to do with it?"

"Take him home and put him in Granddaddy's empty aquarium in my bedroom. Do you think I could put him in your mom's Buick™, to take it home?"

Jack paused before answering. "I don't think that's a good idea at all—it's Mom's brand new car."

"It's either the Buick™ or my mother's fancy lunch basket. You know, he's probably hungry as anything after getting caught. Would you eat anything out of there after he's been eating things in there?"

"Okay. But if we get caught, you're taking the blame!"

Since Jack had sneakers, he headed for the car with the frog. *They'll never blame me, without sneakers,* I thought.

When Jack returned, we saw many older kids screaming about an activity that was going to take place. When we got there, I asked the kid with the crew cut hair what all the excitement was about.

"We're going to play tug of war!"

Jack and I stood watching as the two captains selected teams. When they finished, everyone on each team grabbed the rope, putting a strain on it, and dug their feet into the sand ready for the tug of war to begin.

Mountain Valley Pool (Courtesy Richard Willis)

Miss C, the lifeguard, said, "The game starts when I say go. Is everyone all set?

95

One captain yelled, "No! Get that kid out of the way."

She blew her whistle. I turned and looked at her.

"Yes you," Miss C said, as I backed away from the rope. She blew her whistle again and said, "Ready, set, **GO!**"

The rope went back and forth, participants grunting with all their strength, as though their life depended on this victory. The cheering was incredible from those that watched. I was enthralled and wanted to get my hands on the rope. A little voice in my head said, *"Go help them out."* A moment later, I grabbed the rope, tugging it like crazy, as our team pulled for the conquest, winning the game.

As the winning team congratulated one another, by pats on the back and handshakes, I strutted amongst them with my expanded chest. I looked up at my tall teammates, wearing a million-dollar smile and said, "You guys can thank me for our win! It was my tug that won the game!" Most ignored me, except the one with the crew cut.

"Yeah, little buddy, without you we might have lost!"

Jack came over to me; I thought he was going to congratulate me for helping win the game, but instead said, "When you get to be a teenager like them, don't ever expect to be picked for a team!"

"They're going to be fighting to have me on their team, buddy. You know what that kid just said?...."

****

After the game, I was dripping with sweat and ran to the shallow water with Jack. We mostly fooled around, playing water tag and splashing each other to stay cool. A few times I practiced swimming, using what I learned earlier in the day, but still sank to the bottom each time. I watched with envy, as older teenagers swam effortlessly, wondering what in the world I was doing wrong.

Our mothers called us for lunch, none too soon, Jack and I were starving. Everyone sat on their blankets ready to enjoy lunch. My mother reached for her fancy wood lunch basket when the thought went through my head, *What if Jack chickened out and didn't put the frog into his mother's new car, but put it into my mother's lunch basket instead?*

I dove like a football player to intercept my mother's hands and said, "Let me open it, I want to be a gentleman." My mother looked at me as if I lost my marbles.

"Okay. What kind of mischief have you got into now?" she asked, with a worried look, as she somehow read my mind.

With a smile on my face, I said, "I just want to be a good son." Jack looked at me raising his eyebrows and rolled his eyes.

I flicked the metal latch and opened the lid in slow motion, all the while peeking inside, waiting for the creature to jump out— it didn't. I doubled checked, shuffling sandwiches and snacks around, checking out every inch. I handed Mom her peanut butter and jelly sandwich, then grabbed mine.

After lunch, Jack and I played Checkers ™, while our mothers took a snooze on their blankets with both their kid radars switched on, scanning what we were doing.

When Mom woke up, she glanced at her watch and said it was safe to go back in the water. At this point, we were all drenched in perspiration and headed for the water to cool down. When Mom got in, she mentioned how refreshing the water was. We spent most of the afternoon in the water, with me practicing swimming, taking breaks for soda and snacks.

By the time five o'clock rolled around, we packed our things to leave the pool. Jack and I were still in our bathing suits as our mothers put on what they called cover-ups. "Mom, why do you have to put that thing on? It looks like a Cub Scout camping tent. Why don't you and Mrs. Johnson do what Jack and I do, just wear your bathing suits home—it would be a lot cooler."

"Women, always have to use a cover-up—we need to be modest in public," my mother said, with a serious face.

"Hey Jack, aren't you glad we're boys, and never have to be modest?" I said, with a chuckle.

He agreed.

We headed back, with me carrying the two towels for the cloth walkway to get to the car. Jack and I looked at one another, probably thinking the same thoughts about the frog. *Where would he hide? Would he still be alive without water in a hot car? Would Jack be punished for putting the little guy in there? How long would we be banished to our bedrooms, if we get caught?* I practiced my defense in my head several times, so it would be convincing if Jack blurted out, "It was Greg that did it." *Now, Mrs. Johnson, how could it be me? I don't even have sneakers to get to the car!*

We all arrived at the car, as Mrs. Johnson said, "I thought I closed the windows." Jack looked at me with a guilty expression.

Jack and I cautiously entered the back of the car, looking where we placed our feet and where we placed our butts—it wasn't there, it was nowhere to be seen. I whispered to Jack, "It's got to be in the front with our mothers." He looked at me in horror. We looked at one another and crossed our legs, arms, and fingers—every possible body part, except for our eyes. And maybe we should have done that, too!

Mrs. Johnson exited the parking lot with a happy grin on her face, enjoying the drive with her new car. She made a left and headed up the road. At the flashing red light in the center of town, she made another left heading down East Main Street. She got to where the two churches were and relief flashed in my head: *absolutely nothing can ever go bad near a church, certainly not near two churches.* We almost got past them both, when froggy decided to jump inside Mrs. Johnson's cover-up!

It all happened so fast. She screamed, and then probably meant to hit the brake, but hit the gas pedal instead. The mighty Roadmaster™ took off, and Mrs. Johnson realized her mistake and stomped on the brake causing the car to skid over the curb and onto the grass before coming to an abrupt stop. She glanced out the windshield, with her heart beating in overdrive, when she noticed her new wheel cover rolling down East Main Street.

She immediately slammed the car into park, jumped out without closing the door, and became immodest, ripping the tent off as fast as she could. Then, she looked down at her legs, looking for something.

My mother shot out of the car, too, trying to find out what just happened. "Did you just get stung by a bee?"

"Something slimy got inside my cover-up and slithered against my leg!" she said, shivering.

Mom picked up her cover-up and inspected it. "Nothing's in it. Let me check the car, where you sat."

"See anything?"

"Joan! I found it! There's a frog on your floor mat!"

Mrs. Johnson went to check it out. She left her cover-up on the ground, went over to the car, and screamed, "A damn frog!" She flung open the rear door almost breaking it off its hinges, looked at the both of us, and yelled, "Who put a frog in my car?" She looked at me and asked, "Was it you, Greg?"

I recited my well-practiced line, "It wasn't me! I didn't even wear sneakers today. Maybe it jumped through one of the open car windows."

Her eyes focused on her son. "Jack! Why did you do such a stupid thing?"

I looked at Jack, wondering how he would answer his mother.

"Greg told me to do it!"

With a stern look, detention written on every crease in her frown, Mrs. Johnson said, "Get the damn frog out of the car!"

Even though I was a great frog catcher, it took me forever to catch froggy, especially with an audience watching my every move. When I finally cornered it and grabbed it with two hands, I let it go on the front lawn of the Episcopal Church, hoping it would be safe there, then thought: *Bad things can happen in front of a church. I hope it doesn't get run over.*

It was a silent ride home for Jack and I. He turned now and then and gave me a dirty look as he held the hubcap on his lap with two hands. My mother was the only one talking, profusely apologizing to her friend, promising it would never happen again. Mom was right; Mrs. Johnson never gave us a ride to the pool, ever again.

Arriving home, we said goodbye to the Johnsons. I was immediately sent to my room as punishment. When I got there, I closed the door and walked over to my empty aquarium. It brought great memories of Granddaddy. I stroked my finger along the top metal edge and thought how neat it would have been to have froggy in there. Then the thought floated into my head: *I wonder what else I can capture to put in here next, maybe a turtle?*

****

Mountain Valley Pool served Mendham Borough for many years. Many children took lessons and learned how to swim there. It was a great place to cool off on a hot summer day and play with other children. The pool closed down years later when the water became contaminated and no longer met state quality requirements and later was turned into a park. In the fall of 2017, Mountain Valley Park was drained to make repairs and improvements.

Today, the pool serves as a park, complete with benches and a gazebo that overlooks the two and one-half acre pond for visitors to enjoy its mesmerizing peacefulness. Each May on a given

Saturday, the town has a special event for kids. They stock the pond with trout for children to fish.

This spring I took a ride over there to check the park out. I even found the sandy beach where I learned to do the doggie paddle and failed my swimming test. Yup! The frogs were as noisy as ever, but I didn't get on my hands and knees to try to catch one!

Chapter 10

Davy Crockett

Mendham Borough, NJ 1954

It happened on a November morning when I saw what David wore to school—a ridiculous hat, that no one had seen before.

He arrived in the classroom, just before the eight-o'clock bell sounded, running over to the closet to hang up his coat. I watched him go to his desk and then plopped noisily down in his chair out of breath. A moment later, the hallway bell rang.

Mr. Johnson's sixth-grade class sat in their seats, some slumped over, still half asleep, trying to wake up. A few kids turned their heads to see who arrived so late and saw it was David. We stared in disbelief on the tail protruding from the back of his head. He captured the teacher's attention, too. Mr. Johnson stood in front of his class speechless, staring at David.

Almost immediately, Dorothy broke out with a little chuckle. It was contagious, spreading hilarious laughter throughout the room. Pandemonium broke out shortly after. Charlie, the class clown, got up from his desk, went over to David, and yanked on the hat's bushy tail, almost pulling it off, and then proceeded to wag it back and forth like a happy puppy dog.

"Where did your father shoot this thing?" Charlie asked.

"He didn't shoot it! My mom and dad bought it—it's my birthday present!" David retorted sharply, embarrassed and insulted at the same time.

"No way!" Charlie said, laughing like mad, as he gave it another yank before returning to his desk.

103

With the classroom still in chaos, Mr. Johnson walked over to David to get a closer look. He couldn't resist either and gave the tail a gentle pull and said, "Put it away in the closet."

"I'm sorry, Mr. Johnson, if I do that, one of the kids will steal it on me."

"Then give it to me," Mr. Johnson said, as David handed it over. He carried the coonskin hat up to his desk and placed it down on a stack of papers in the corner. He then began his lesson plan. As he picked up a piece of white chalk and outlined some important battles during the War of Independence on the blackboard, we listened, but our eyes and minds were glued to the dead raccoon sitting on his desk.

When lunchtime arrived, I thought David made a big mistake. He retrieved his hat from Mr. Johnson's desk, placed it on his head, and headed for the basement cafeteria, two flights down. I saw David place his foot on the first step to go down the stairs. Charlie grabbed his hat by the tail and gave it a hard yank. To his horror, the tail broke off. He glanced momentarily at the hatless tail in his hand, then raced down the stairs for the cafeteria with David in hot pursuit.

"Got your stupid coon tail! Got your stupid coon tail!" he shouted to David as he ran.

From the stairway landing, I saw Charlie stuff the tail into his front pocket before David caught-up with him in the cafeteria.

"Give me back my tail! My mother's going to have a fit when she sees what you've done to my hat!

Charlie refused to return the tail and a fight broke out. I stood there watching them wrestling on the floor yelling and screaming over the tail at each other. They got Mrs. Waters attention. She was in charge of the cafeteria and prepared all the meals. She ran over to the fight.

"Break it up or you're both going to the office!" she screamed, holding a serving spoon in her hand, shaking it at them.

They both quit fighting and got up when they heard her say 'office.' It was the word of fear and doom and synonymous with the name Latterlee—Principal Latterlee.

Charlie got in the lunch-line first, with a part of the tail peeking out from his front pants pocket. I was standing behind when I saw David try to grab it, but Charlie was faster, turning his body away. Moments later, David placed his hand roughly on Charlie's shoulder and yelled in his ear, "Give me the tail!"

An argument began once again, along with some pushing and shoving, as Charlie egged David on, singing repeatedly; "Davy Crockett with the tailless hat, couldn't shoot his musket for a pile of crap!"

"You, give me back my tail!" David shouted, shaking his closed fist.

"Hey! You two! Cut it out, or you'll both be having lunch with Mr. Latterlee," Mrs. Waters warned, once again.

Fearing the tailless hat would be taken again, David took it off and held it securely against his chest on his way to the table. By this time, teachers started arriving for their lunch, too. They had a special room that afforded them some peace and quiet, away from the kids.

The entrance door to the cafeteria opened again. This time, I saw it wasn't a teacher, but the infamous Mr. Latterlee, the feared principal. The loud chatter and laughing stopped instantly, like turning off a radio in the middle of a blasting hit tune. The kids' eyes focused on him standing by the doorway. Mr. Dreadful, the enforcer, the man with one stroke of his pen that could expel you or worse yet, make you repeat a grade.

I watched as he scanned every table, looking for that guilty kid. This day would be a day the poor kid would always remember. His eyes landed on our table with David sitting next to me. He began walking to our table with his large black olive-sized eyes peering through those thick frameless glasses. I got nervous, thinking he might want me.

When he got to our table, he stood directly behind David's chair looking down at him, not saying a word.

David lowered his shoulders and hunched over hoping somehow Mr. Latterlee would go away, perhaps go to another table. A few moments later, I glanced at David as he inconspicuously turned his head, peered down, and saw the brown suit trousers and large brown wing-tipped shoes. He knew that wasn't going to happen.

Latterlee liked to see a problem kid sweat a little. He knew just how tight to pull their string of fear. He waited in silence until he saw the kid's face blush crimson red or maybe a little longer when beads of perspiration began forming. On one or two occasions, he got a kid so nervous that he peed himself and had to be sent home. David's face had blushed as Mr. Latterlee commanded, "Give me the Davy Crockett's hat, David. It's causing too much trouble here in school."

He lifted his butt and pulled out the coonskin hat that he had been sitting on. Mr. Latterlee inspected the hat briefly and asked, "Where's the tail?"

"Charlie's got it. He pulled it off!"

Mr. Latterlee walked over to the next table where Charlie sat, tapped him on the shoulder, and said, "Hand it over."

Charlie slipped his hand in his pocket, pulled out the tail, and placed it into the large waiting hand.

Mr. Latterlee turned and walked back to our table and said to David, "Nice hat, but a terrible disturbance for the school. Come to the office at the end of the day and you can wear it back home, but don't wear it to school again," he warned, as he walked back to his office.

The kids started to giggle. It looked silly seeing him carrying the hat in one hand and the tail draping in the other. After the door slammed closed, an explosion of bottled up laughter broke-out. It was a way for kids to release all their tension of the moment.

It got so loud, that Mrs. Waters grabbed one of her biggest pots and a mixing spoon, walked out to the table area, and began beating the bottom of the pot. The loud drumming noise immediately ended the out of control laughter.

At the end of the school day, David headed for the dreaded school office—the last place a kid wanted to be. He walked nervously up to the school's secretary, Miss Maples, sitting behind her desk, typing a million keystrokes per minute on her Royal typewriter. Her fingers stopped, as she turned to look at David. "May I help you, David?" she asked.

"I want my hat back."

"Sure—the one with the broken furry tail," she said with a chuckle.

When David got home, he threw the hat and tail on the kitchen table and announced to his mother who was reading a recipe, "I'm never going to wear this hat again! I knew it was stupid when you gave it to me! Who wears a dead raccoon on their head anyway?"

"It's not stupid!" his mother replied. "It's a Davy Crockett hat."

"You don't have any idea what trouble it caused today. First, all the kids laughed at it, like a bunch of hyenas, then Mr. Johnson took it away. If that wasn't bad enough, Charlie pulled the tail off it at lunchtime! Then, I went to lunch and that scary principal, Mr. Latterlee took it away from me, then got the tail from Charlie. He brought them to the office, his private office. He banned me from ever bringing it to school again."

"We'll see about that! He has no right telling kids what they can wear and can't wear to school.

"You got that wrong, Mom. He's Mr. Latterlee, everybody's afraid of him, even the teachers.

The next morning, I saw David come into the classroom hatless. He was running late again.

The kids, at their desks, hearing other kids tease him on his way in, turned around with disappointment seeing he wasn't wearing his coonskin hat. They wanted to join in on the fun as well.

Within a month, almost all of us had one, even Charlie. David's mother did speak to Mr. Latterlee and David was given permission to wear the hat to school as long he checked it in the office each morning. Kids, knowing the rule for David's hat, handed theirs in, too. It didn't take long before Miss Maples knocked on Mr. Latterlee's door.

"Excuse me, Mr. Latterlee. May I have a word with you about these Davy Crocket hats?"

"Sure, what's the problem?"

"They're stinking up the office, especially on a rainy day. Secondly, there are so many of them, I've run out of room to store them. At the end of the day, it takes me forever to locate a pupil's hat. With all these hats, we need to hire a part-time hat checker!"

"I see your point, Mary. I wondered what this odor was looming in our office."

The next day, a notice was placed in all the teachers' mail slots to read to the students the following day.

"Due to the popularity of Davy Crocket hats, these hats will now be permitted to be worn to school and kept in the classroom as long as they have a nametag." Signed, William G. Latterlee.

The hats were wonderful. They kept you warm during recess and traveling to and from school. This fad only lasted about two years when they lost their popularity, including mine. Interesting enough, they can be bought today, even for adults.

Our graduating class wanted to give Mr. Latterlee a parting gift upon our 1956 June graduation. Can you guess what we wanted to package up for him? Our homeroom teacher set us straight and changed our mind. "You know he has that powerful pen of doom and can keep you all back for another year."

Charlie, our class clown, stood up and said, "Why don't we give him a bag of marbles!

****

For a number of weeks, Walt Disney, a famous producer, aired episodes of "Davy Crockett," who dressed in early settlers outdoor clothing including a coonskin hat. It became a fad— every kid across the country wanted one, and that included younger children in Mendham.

Chapter 11

Mendham's First Dental Practice

Mendham Borough, NJ 1955

I had just started seventh grade and I began my walk home after school, down East Main Street. I saw a guy hanging-up a brand new sign in front of a small building, four houses down from Robinson's Drug Store in the center of town. As I neared the sign, it read MENDHAM DENTAL PRACTICE with DR. BENNETT, DDS underneath. I didn't give it a second thought. Arriving home with several books under my arm, I plopped them down on the kitchen table, one of those with a Formica™ top with a wide metal decorative band wrapped around the edge.

"Hi, Mom!" I said. My mother was peeling carrots in the kitchen sink for dinner.

"How was school today?"

"It really was a fun day. We had an assembly program with a magician doing tricks. We had front row seats, too. You remember how scary Mr. Latterlee is, well today he was even scarier, looking at us through those thick glasses and with an angry look. He assigned our class these seats as punishment for last year's marble rolling contest. Several of the boys in my class had dropped dozens of marbles on the floor during an assembly movie, seeing who's made the most noise rolling down the steep floor clanging against the metal chairs.

"I hope you didn't do that?"

"Billy felt sorry for me because I didn't have any marbles and gave me a few of his."

"You know better than to do that!"

"I thought of that after I dropped them, Mom. Getting back to Mr. Latterlee, he was still mad from last year.

Can you believe that? He kept that stored in his brain from last year, no wonder he's lost most of his hair! He escorted our class into the auditorium and marched us right down to the first two rows. The kids from the other classes were clapping and laughing their brains out watching us follow Mr. Latterlee to our seats. He turned and gave them a stern look and told them to be quiet. 'Enjoy the show,' he said to us, rubbing his hands together. I read his lips and under his breath he mouthed, 'Problem solved,' then dipped his head."

"Well, with all the shenanigans your classmates pulled-off last year, he made a wise decision," Mom said.

"Not really."

"Why?" Mom asked.

"Being so close to the stage, every time the magician went to do a trick, one of the class wise-guys would shout out, 'I saw how you did that trick!'"

"That wasn't too nice for the younger children in the lower grades who were probably enjoying his magic tricks."

"It happened four times, it got the magician really nervous and on edge. He was about ready to do the rabbit in the hat trick when the rabbit must have gotten nervous, too—it came shooting out from his sleeve and ran off-stage. Some of the little kids in the audience started crying, they were really upset. Our class went into hysterics, yelling, screaming, and stomping our feet. They screamed, 'Go rabbit! Go rabbit!' Then Barry yelled out, 'Now we know where you hide the rabbit!' That's when Mr. Latterlee zoomed down the aisle and grabbed Barry by the collar for detention in his office."

"Well, that sounds like quite a day. Would you like a root beer float?"

"Yeah, but let it warm-up. Cold stuff gives me a toothache these days."

"The *Mendham Gazette* had an article about a dental practice starting-up on Main Street."

"Well, that's stupid! Why would anyone want to go to a dentist that is still practicing?"

"That's the lingo that doctors and dentists use when they describe their medical business."

"That still seems really strange to me using the word practice."

It was ten minutes later when I put the spoon of vanilla ice cream in my mouth that it happened. "**OW!** Mom, I've got an awful toothache." I dropped the spoon and put my thumb in my mouth over the bad tooth to quench the sharp throbbing pain.

"I'm going to call him right now to make an appointment so he can look at that tooth."

"No way! I don't want to go! I'm not going to a dentist that's still practicing!"

Mom got me the earliest appointment to see the dentist after school. The next day, she walked all the way from home, about a mile away, to meet me at his office. Dr. Bennett greeted us with a friendly smile. He wasn't at all scary, like most doctors. He looked much younger than my mom, about average height, wore glasses, and had a mustache. He had on a starched blue shirt with those buttons on top of the shoulders and beige slacks. He asked my mother to wait in the waiting room while he examined my teeth.

"Sit right here in this chair, Greg."

I hesitated and checked-out the chair. I had never seen a dental chair before. It was a chair made of leather and steel, one that would leave no pleasant memory, I was sure. I cautiously sat down and scanned all the dentist's equipment, along with the tray of sharp metal pokers and the miniature mirror with the small handle. The tension inside me kept building up as my knees jiggled sideways like strings on a fiddle, so much so that I crossed my legs to keep them still.

113

"First time you've seen a dentist, Greg?"

"Yeah, how did you guess?"

"Your knees. I'll be gentle and get rid of that awful toothache."

Dr. Bennett smiled as he tipped me back in the chair and adjusted the large dental light above me that sort of blinded me.

"Open your mouth, Greg."

He picked up his sharp metal probe and began poking at my first tooth.

"You can close your mouth now, I need to make a note on your chart."

He continued to go from tooth to tooth, stopping frequently to add more notes to his chart. It seemed to take him forever to finish. I was keeping count of how many times he made a note—fourteen times. The last tooth, he kept examining and poking at for a long while. He called my mother into the examination room.

"Mrs. Smith, your son has fourteen cavities and a molar that is severely decayed. It needs to be extracted. He'll need to see an oral surgeon for that procedure."

"Oh my gosh! No wonder the poor kid's had so many toothaches! Let's make an appointment to start his dental work, right away. I'll need to budget money for all this. How much will it cost?"

While they discussed the dental fees, I sat in the chair as fear and panic bounced around in my head. *Fourteen cavities, oral surgery, tooth extraction.* My head was spinning with all the gloom and doom I had just heard.

"I can see him tomorrow, after school," Dr. Bennett said with a smile.

I was scared to death. I thought about my dental disaster and what would happen on my first visit. Mom and I walked the long-distance home to find a way to avoid the drill and the pliers.

"It'll be alright. He'll give you something for the pain while he drills-out the decay in your teeth."

"PAIN? DRILL? Mom, that sounds like torture!"

"He told me he was an Air Force Oral Surgeon, Hon; he has had lots of experience."

"Well, I'm no Air Force guy! I'm just a kid, a 7th grader!"

That night, as I had just fallen asleep, my nightmare began. It was a doozy. Dr. Bennett put the wrong size bit in his drill and drilled half my tooth away before he realized it, saying, "Here's another tooth for the oral surgeon."

Alarmed, I screamed, "Why did you do that, you idiot?"

He laughed and said, "Just practicing. I make those mistakes all the time, but I'm just practicing."

I woke up with my entire body ringing wet with sweat and tried to go back to sleep. I couldn't. I watched the dials on Little Ben, my alarm clock, go by, hour by hour.

After getting up and feeling sick to my stomach the next morning, I skipped breakfast and headed for my walk to school with my books under one arm and carrying my brown bag lunch in the other. Arriving at school, I had hoped that my classes would drag out forever, to delay my visit with Dr. Bennett— unfortunately, they didn't.

The three-fifteen bell rang and I was headed to see him. Scared to death, I needed a distraction on the walk there. I stared down at the sidewalk slates, counting each one, as I proceeded to his front walk—I counted thirty-six. I didn't know why I did the counting, maybe to distract me for what was to come. I entered the waiting room alone, without Mom. *I've got to be brave and man-up, even if I'm just a 7th grader.* I sat down in the chair in the waiting room. He must have heard me because a few moments later, the door opened with a click.

"You can come in now, Greg. How was your day at school?"

I wanted to tell him the truth, "scared to death," as my heart raced ready to burst out of my chest. But I manned up and said, "Good."

He asked me to sit in the steel and leather chair as he sat in front of me on a small stool and began talking to me about my hobbies and sports. I told him that I was lousy at sports but good at inventing stuff. I told him all about the X-ray machine my friends and I built along with all the experiments we did with electronics.

"My pals and I can build an X-ray machine for you, too, Dr. Bennett."

"No, no, I don't think that's a very good idea."

We were deep in conversation when he suddenly tipped the dental chair way back and adjusted the lamp. He turned so his back was facing me. I moved in the chair trying to look around him to see what he was up to, but he blocked my vision. Before I knew it, he turned around holding a humongous metal syringe in his hand.

"Open-up. This is going to feel like a little pinch."

He stuck it in me. My eyes nearly popped out of my head, expecting a pinch and got a stabbing. *Lie number one!* He slowly jabbed me in several other places around my tooth.

"Rinse," he said, as I saw him put a drill in his drilling machine that was mounted on a long arm.

"Do you have the right size drill?" I asked.

He turned, looked at me strangely, and said, "Of course."

"I just wanted to make sure, Dr. Bennett. Mom said you had a practice here."

He looked at me with an odd expression and told me to rest, he'd be back in fifteen minutes. *Rest, you got to be kidding!* After he stepped out, I sat up in the chair and started a frightful inspection of all his equipment.

116

I didn't get too far until my jello knees started jiggling side to side again. They seemed to be telling me, 'I don't want to be here.' He almost caught me double-checking the size of the miniature drill that he had installed in the drill machine as I held it in my hand. Once I heard his footsteps, I quickly hung it up on the holder.

He came into the room and asked, "Numb?"

I thought he had said, "Dumb?" *Yeah, for being in this damn chair!*

"I can't feel my lips anymore," I tried to tell him in a strange, distorted voice. My fingers touched my lips to make sure that they were still there.

"That's good, I'll start to take out the decay in your tooth."

I sat there in horror, as I watched a huge round belt on the drill going a zillion miles an hour, stop, and start-up again. I could smell the awful odor of my tooth burning-up as he drilled. He stopped and used a miniature squirt gun on a hose to dowse my tooth with water to put out the fire. When he went to grab the drill again, I felt the huge hole in my tooth with my tongue and wondered if we had both erred and he was using a drill that was too big.

"It feels like you drilled half the tooth away," I said.

Completely ignoring me, he said, "Open."

He was back at it for more drilling to make the hole bigger, squirting water each time until he hung up his drill. He started mixing some silver stuff together.

"What's that?" I asked.

"Amalgamated Mercury, filling material."

"I know what Mercury is. We play around with it at school, rolling the liquid Mercury beads around on the classroom floor. My friends and I used Mercury vapor in our X-ray tube, too."

"Open," he said, as he packed the stuff into the huge hole in my tooth. He continued to use his little tools to fill and pack the tooth, then cleaned the excess off with a piece of cotton and a pair of tweezers.

"Your tooth is fixed, see you next week."

For several weeks, I continued to see Dr. Bennett and got used to everything but the metal syringe. It seemed to me he played a version of dental hide and seek with the syringe. Fortunately, he won each visit, hiding it well.

On my last appointment, after he filled my last tooth, Dr. Bennett said with a smile, "You were a great patient, Greg."

I looked back at him with a proud smile and replied, "You can change your sign now, Dr. Bennett."

"What do you mean?" he asked, looking at me.

"After fixing all my teeth, you won't be practicing anymore."

Chapter 12

"I should've kept my mouth shut!"

Mendham Borough, NJ 1955

My bad tooth became more of a problem, even after all the weeks of dental treatment with Dr. Bennett, but this one he couldn't help me with, it had to be extracted.

****

Thursday, I complained to Mom, "Mom, this tooth hurts all the time now. Look how my right cheek is swollen and all puffed out. It hurts when I touch it."

"We're going to have someone look at it right away." Mom replied.

The following Saturday morning, my dad yelled down the stairs to my lab in the basement, "We've got to take a ride to Morristown."

"Why Dad? I'm right in the middle of taking apart an old radio." Begrudgingly, I turned off my soldering iron, picked up my stack of graham crackers and milk and headed outside. He was parked in front of our house. Dad sat behind the wheel with the car running, ready to go until he spotted the milk and crackers. He jumped out of the car and started yelling.

"You know what the rule is! Absolutely no food or drinks in this car. I can't have business customers sitting on a soiled seat with graham cracker crumbs all over the place."

"Come on Dad! I was working so hard on that radio that I forgot to eat my morning snack."

"Put those back in the house and you can have them later."

I opened the car door, ran to the front door, and rang the bell. Mom opened the door and I handed her my snack and drink. "This stinks Mom! Dad won't let me have these in the car."

"Your dad is very particular in keeping his car immaculate. He has to. He entertains customers, taking them out to lunch."

"Well, today he could entertain me, his kid!"

"Can't you tell me why I have to come with you today?" Dad didn't answer right away. He put the car in drive and we were on our way, wherever that was.

We were on Mendham Road, heading towards Morristown when he replied to my question. "You have an appointment to have an oral surgeon extract your tooth, the one that's been giving you a toothache."

It hit me like a ton of bricks. I was going in for oral surgery. *The doc is going to yank it out with pliers! Gotta get out of this— now!* With a shaky voice, I said to Dad, "The tooth is fine, Dad. You can turn around and go back home."

"It's got to come out, it might even be abscessed. It's only going to get worse."

Hearing that, I wanted to jump out of the car. My hand reached for the door handle, ready to make the jump. But, one glance over at the speedometer with the needle stuck at forty, I knew that was not an option, I'd kill myself. I removed my hand from the lever and sat frozen in a state of fear.

Seeing how upset I was, Dad said to comfort me, "They'll give you some gas that will put you to sleep. You won't feel a thing."

"They're going to gas me? How are they going to do that?"

"The nurse will just place a mask over your mouth and nose. You'll just smell a sweet aroma and then fall peacefully asleep."

This is the worst day of my life, maybe I should make the jump.

After arriving in Morristown, we parked the car and entered the Park Avenue office building near the town square.

Dad led me to the elevator. We entered it and he pushed button 3. It lit and we took off like a spaceship for the third floor. Feeling sick to my stomach, I almost left my breakfast on the third floor when it came to an abrupt stop. The doors opened and we walked out.

"Are you okay? You look kind of pale," Dad said.

"Not really. I almost lost my breakfast back there in the elevator."

We walked down a long hall. I could smell the dental surgery office even before we got to it. It's that putrid antiseptic smell. This smelled worse, maybe it had that ether stuff mixed in. We got to the door with the words Dr. Gaulic, Dental Surgeon stenciled in big black lettering on the frosted glass door. *They frost the glass so people can't see what horrible things go on in there.* My legs started shaking like strings on a bass fiddle. We sat down in the waiting room. My head was going crazy with apprehension, fearing being knocked out, and having my tooth yanked out. The shaking spread to my arms and jaws. My teeth were clattering against one another making such a racket that the woman sitting across from us, peeked over her *Look* magazine to see where the noise was coming from.

The surgery door opened with a click and the nurse peeked out and said, "Gregory Smith."

Dad looked over at me, gave me a pat on the back, and said, "Don't be nervous."

The woman with the *Look* magazine peeked again at me with a sorrowful expression as I headed for the door of doom with my head hung low. My father was watching me too. I turned and said, "Want to change places, Dad? We'll see if your legs wobble and teeth chatter like a sewing machine."

Hearing this, the nurse said to him, "Do you want to come in with your son?"

"Sure," he said and followed me through the door.

Dad stood in the back of the surgical operating suite as the nurse told me to sit in the dental chair. This one was like Dr. Bennett's, except it had leather straps. My eyes nearly popped out of my head when I noticed them hanging from the arms and the back of the chair. I just stood there in panic mode trying to come up with some rational reason why they needed leather straps.

"Please, sit down on the chair," the nurse said.

I didn't want to sit down. I stood frozen in fear.

"Sit in the chair," the nurse commanded.

As I sat down, I saw the steel hammer, pliers, and chisel placed on a tray near me. I was ready to run. But turning my head, I could see my dad standing in the doorway blocking my way. I could hear the nurse fiddling around with something behind me and then a hiss of gas. Two seconds later, she put the black rubber mask over my face.

This isn't sweet. It's awful! I can't breathe! She wasn't ready for my reaction. I turned my head and pushed the mask away. "I can't breathe! I can't breathe! She's killing me, Dad! I turned my head to ask my father to save me. I saw him take one-step towards me, then faint, falling hard, face down on the floor.

I've got to get out of here or I'll die!

That's when all hell broke loose. I was a big kid for my age and had grown strong from all my yard work and I fought back. There were four hands on the mask, two of mine and two of hers. The doctor wanted to add two more, but I head-butted him right in the gut. His hands went there to ease his pain.

"Uh!" he yelled.

He looked at me with a vengeance as I rose partially out of the chair, leaving the nurse holding the hissing mask. I tried to get completely up from the chair, but the doc pushed me back.

"Strap him down!" shouted the doctor while he held me in the chair.

122

The nurse struggled to secure the straps tightly over my arms as I tried to fight them off.

I twisted my arms as best I could to avoid the grasp of the leather strap. She managed to get my left arm tight to the armrest. I swung my right arm trying to miss her clawing hands, but she was faster than me pulling that strap tight against the other armrest.

I was going to head-butt him again, but she killed that chance when she strapped my chest to the chair. I was on my own to battle the evil dental team.

"Get some smelling salts and tend to the father!" Dr. Gaulic shouted.

Psyched-up in a fight for my life, I heard the nurse slide a drawer open with a bang and heard her run over to my father. As I turned my head, I saw him sprawled out on the floor with blood oozing from his nose.

By this time, I could smell the ether filling the room. Dr. Gaulic must have smelled it too. Moments later, he had the mask in his hand and was going to plaster it to my face.

But, they forgot to strap one part of me—my legs. I started kicking anything and everything in sight, including the doctor, but that didn't save me. He grabbed my legs and held them as tight as a metal vise. Then came the two words that escalated my fear.

"Gas him!" Dr. Gaulic shouted.

She grabbed the mask and forcefully plastered it to my face. I struggled to breathe, yanking my head left, then right. I felt like I was going to die. I couldn't get any air, just an awful smelly gas and then everything went black.

Sometime later, they removed my arm straps. For a second my eyes blinked open, then closed and my head fell to my chest. I felt hard slaps striking me in my face, as I struggled to open my eyes.

To my horror, there was the nurse slapping me; first on the left and then on the right side of my face. I didn't know why she was doing this. Probably punishment for head-butting Dr. Gaulic and fighting her off. *Defend yourself!* Fighting for my life again, I started smacking her back with both hands until the referee, Dr. Gaulic, broke up our free-for-all. He grabbed my wrists and yelled, "Stop it!" I felt the wad of cotton inside my mouth and tasted the coppery blood shooting out where my tooth had been. I kept swallowing it; there was so much that some even trickled out of my mouth.

The doctor roughly pulled me out of the chair with an angry stare in his eyes. Still dizzy, I shuffled to the waiting room hating both of them, thinking about how I could get even. I saw my father sitting in a chair with black and blue marks all over his face. He was waving a little capsule back and forth under his nose. He looked awful. My dad was always tan because he spent so much time outside in the yard, but now, he was as white as a sheet of paper.

"Are you okay to drive?" the nurse asked him.

My father glanced over at me and gave me a dirty look like this whole disaster was my fault. "Yeah, I'll be okay."

I walked over to him, looking like a boxer who lost his fight, as droplets of blood trickled down my lip. "You should have driven me home, Dad, when I asked you to."

It started out as a quiet ride back to Mendham; that was until I had to puke. My father could not pull over fast enough, as my stomach erupted in protest to the ether.

You can imagine his horror of seeing me puke all over my seat! The worst part, being so fastidious, he had nothing in his car to clean up the mess. So we had to drive home in that awful stench. It was so bad that I thought he was going to puke himself as I saw him continuously gag.

After a few hundred feet, Dad was able to get over to the side of the road and park safely. He went from door to door cranking down each window.

124

We drove off again with Dad's head leaning out his driver's side window for some fresh air to keep him from puking too or worse yet, fainting. We got a mile up the road when round two occurred. "Dad! I'm going to throw-up again!"

This time, Dad drove to the side of the road like a racecar driver, just in time for me to swing my door open. I was on my knees in a split second, and let me tell you, I wasn't praying. I had never felt so sick in my life. I emptied my stomach again and we set off once more for home. After our perilous ride, we pulled into our circular driveway and stumbled through the front door to our living room.

My mother was there waiting, concerned for my well-being after the procedure. One look at the two of us and she was ready to faint too! Dad's face was all black and blue, still white as a sheet of paper and I reeked of puke.

"What happened to the two of you?"

I headed for the couch and Dad plopped down in the first chair he found in the living room.

"You look like you two were in a brawl!" Mom said with alarm.

"I don't know where to begin," Dad said.

Dad spent the rest of the weekend cleaning the inside of the car with every soap detergent he could find around the house. When that didn't work, he headed for the haunted barn to find some of the heavy-duty stuff.

It was late Sunday afternoon when he came into the house with a disgusted look on his face.

"The damn car still smells like puke," he angrily complained to my mother. "How am I ever going to entertain clients in this car?"

"Why don't you sprinkle some of that Old Spice™ aftershave inside the car?" Mom suggested.

Dad looked at my mom like she was nuts, but soon headed for the bathroom for the Old Spice™.

For me, I got rid of the smell of puke, but the taste of ether lasted several days. The fear of anesthesia was locked inside my brain forever.

The following December, I went Christmas shopping at Robinson's Drug Store, to find some inexpensive gifts for my parents. I bought Mom some perfume and aftershave for Dad. I never gave it a second thought as I picked up his favorite, Old Spice™.

On Christmas morning, I raced into the living room to get my wrapped presents for my parents. I gave Mom hers first, saying, "Merry Christmas, Mom!"

Mom gave me a big hug and said, "You didn't have to buy us gifts. You are so thoughtful. She unwrapped hers with the silver bow. Opened the bottle and took a whiff. This fragrance is wonderful. I'm going to dab some on this afternoon for our family Christmas get together. Thank you, Hon."

"Here Dad, I know you're going to like this, "Merry Christmas!"

Dad unwrapped his gift with a thankful smile. He looked at the Old Spice™ box, then opened it, pulling out the cream-colored bottle with Old Spice in big blue letters on the front. He hesitated, looked at me then the bottle, probably trying to decide what to say. With a confused look, he patted me on my shoulder and asked, "Is this for me or for my car?"

Chapter 13

Our Maine Vacation,

How I Nailed a Movie Star

Mendham Borough, NJ 1955

August rolled around and it was time for our family vacation. Last year my parents had sold their summer home at Lake Hopatcong in Sussex County, New Jersey. For vacation this year they decided to visit the state of Maine, staying at Homewood Inn in Yarmouth, on Casco Bay. For me, it would be my first time to visit Maine; I had no idea what it would be like. The only thing I knew, it was a long car trip according to Dad, one that I was not looking forward to since I was susceptible to getting carsick—really sick.

Friday afternoon before our trip, Dad and I needed to pack our station wagon, a classy 57 Chevy Nomad. Our suitcases were all placed in one area of the living room along with my fishing rod, binoculars, soda, candy, snacks, and a handgun.

Yup, I managed to get a real gun, with my father's approval, as my birthday present in July. Now let me tell you that took lots of planning to make that happen. This gun didn't use shells like my brother's .38 filled with gunpowder. It shot .22 caliber pellets, propelled from compressed CO_2, from a cartridge. It fired pellets as fast as you could pull the trigger with enough power to kill small animals or go through a thin board. The gun looked and felt like a military pistol.

This is how I manipulated my dad into buying the gun for me. That happened after my buddies, Al and Sam, got their powerful .22 caliber pellet rifle for Christmas. With this particular rifle, you had to use a lever to pump air to a chamber to propel the lead pellet.

The speed, distance, and power were proportional to the number of pumps. After letting me fire a few shots, I was hooked and wanted one of my own.

Staying out of mischief for some time and finishing 7th grade with an excellent report card, I couldn't have a better time to ask my dad for a handgun. My .22 caliber rifle had been mysteriously seized, probably by my dad, and I was left with a useless kiddie cork gun. Although, it did kill the bird that used to pop out of our expensive Black Forest cuckoo clock.

Because my parents had me late in life, they were ancient in age compared to my classmates' parents. Other dads had hair on their heads, my dad only had a few strands. He often claimed it was caused by tension and anxiety from all my wild experiments and being mischievous at times.

My dad had a bad heart, and I always worried that he would die from working hard on our property. So, I always worked by his side, doing as many tasks as I could. When I got to fifth grade, I was cutting all the lawns at both houses and around the barns. It took me most of the week to do that. I figured I had to do something more significant than cut lawns, like a big project, to butter him up to ask for a gun.

It was a sunny Saturday morning, early in June, when I headed outside to see what Dad was up to. It didn't take me long to find him. He was standing high on a gigantic metal ladder with a paintbrush in his hand, painting the large red barn. I walked over to ask if I could help.

"Dad, it's going to take you ages to paint this big barn by yourself, can I help you?"

"That's really nice of your son, to offer. You've never painted before, you just don't slap paint on. You have to properly apply it."

"If you show me how, I'll apply it just like you want."

"Okay, you'll need to put on old clothes."

128

"I'll be back in a few minutes, Dad." I ran back to the house to change.

A few minutes later I was back. Dad came down the ladder holding the can of paint and brush. After several minutes of instruction, I had a four-inch brush in my hand, ready to dip into the second can of Sherwin-Williams™ barn-red paint. Before I started, I read the instructions on the label to see if the paint could be used on haunted barns. "Dad, I've got some bad news for you."

"Okay, shoot, what is it?"

"I just read the instructions on the can. It doesn't say anything about using it on haunted barns."

"Do you really think this barn is haunted?"

"You're darn tooten' I do. If you don't believe me, ask Al or Sam," I said, as I picked up my brush and began to paint.

Dad was on the ladder painting while I painted the lower clapboard siding. I could see him glance down occasionally, making sure I was following his instructions.

"How am I doing?"

"Looks good. Make sure you put on enough paint."

I dipped the brush into the can to fill it with paint. I pulled the brush out quickly, to apply more paint on the siding. When I looked down, I noticed that I had dripped paint all over my jeans. *Oh well, Dad can't say I didn't put enough paint on.*

It was after we finished painting that day that I planned to ask him to buy me a real gun for my upcoming birthday. We had just finished cleaning our brushes and hands with turpentine and headed back to the house. Inside, Dad opened the refrigerator, grabbed a can of beer for himself and a bottle of soda for me.

"Thanks, Dad." I took the ice-cold bottle and went to my room to get my cork gun.

Dad was sitting in the sunroom, in his comfortable chair, relaxing and taking a sip when I came in holding the kiddie gun.

"Dad?"

"Yeah."

"Do you think this gun is appropriate for a kid my age?"

"Probably not. I thought you were only interested in building radios, not shooting guns."

"Al and Sam's parents bought them a pellet rifle. I want a gun, too. A handgun, like the one Walter straps to his belt every day."

"Forget that! No way you're getting a .38 revolver."

"Not a .38 Dad! A pellet gun. You can get one at Sears, through the mail."

"We'll see."

This was my least favorite parental answer—it meant no.

****

It was Friday afternoon when I started to help Dad pack the car for our Maine vacation. I had handed him the last two suitcases when I found out "we'll see" could mean something else.

"Oh, by the way, I have a surprise for you."

"What's that Dad? A new fishing rod?"

"Come on inside."

He went into their bedroom and came back with a box. I had to look twice. There it was, clearly marked on the cardboard box, 'Crossman™ Pellet Gun.' I opened the box and held it carefully in my right hand. After inspecting it in every conceivable way, I pointed it at the once expensive cuckoo clock, without the bird, through the V notch sight and yelled, "POW!"

"Do that again, and it'll be put away until next year!" Dad warned.

"Sorry, Dad, this is so neat, thank you," I said, hugging him. "Can I shoot it? Shoot it now?"

"No, you'll have to wait till we get to Maine. I can't carry a loaded gun in the car. You can shoot it out over the water when we get there."

"May I keep it in my room overnight?"

"No, I'm packing it in the car now, it'll be safer there."

We got up at 4:30 the next morning, had a quick breakfast and got on the road at five. Dad insisted that I ride shotgun. He said it would help me from getting motion sickness. He also assigned me a task, to hand him toll money, probably to take my mind off getting carsick. We got to Connecticut when I shot another one of Dad's theories down the tubes. Dad was taking a curve at sixty when I felt like I was going to throw up. I stuck my head out the open window and emptied my stomach with an awful growl. It was unfortunate for the guy in the hotrod convertible that had been tailgating us for some time. Dad was really getting upset with the guy; threatening to jam on his brakes to teach him a lesson. Whatever was in me was now splattered across the hotrod's windshield, forcing the guy to hit his brakes and head for the shoulder of the road.

I'm sure my dad was counting down the miles in his head before we got to our destination. More episodes followed with me getting sicker. I got so sick that Mom switched places with me. She rode shotgun and I rode laying across the back seat in agony, thinking I was going to die.

After several forced stops, we finally arrived at Homewood Inn in Maine. Dad checked in at the office and we drove to what they called the boathouse. It was a small two-bedroom house with a fireplace that sat on a wooden barge-type flotation platform. Just what I needed! A rocking house to get seasick in, on top of car sickness. There were two steel safety cables that tethered the cottage to large boulders. To get to the house you had to walk down a hinged stairway with railings on both sides.

The walkway had to be hinged to gain access to the house since the tide would rise and fall in excess of eighteen feet.

Feeling like death warmed over, I headed down the gangplank carrying my suitcase for the cottage. I opened the door and headed straight for the closest bedroom, pulled down the shades, and collapsed on the bed. When dinnertime rolled around, Mom and Dad asked if I was hungry.

"Are you feeling any better?" Mom asked.

"No, Mom. I've got a splitting headache and still feel sick to my stomach."

"I'll bring you back some ginger ale™."

They went to the dining hall and I went back to sleep. The next morning, I felt much better. I was always an early riser. The Huck-Finn spirit kicked in and I went off to explore the shores of Casco Bay. It was high tide, an easy exit over the now almost level gangplank to terra firma. I walked with the binoculars in my hand following the rocky coastline when I saw the dog sitting on a boulder, out in the bay surrounded by water. *What's that poor dog doing stranded there?* As I neared, the dog plopped in the water, and never came up. *Oh, the poor thing, he's going to drown! I've got to get Dad to help me rescue him!*

I ran as fast as I could, back to the cabin to get my Dad, to save the dog. I opened their bedroom door without even knocking—it was an emergency!

"Dad! Dad! Wake-up! A dog is drowning!" I screamed, shaking him hard. For a second, I felt bad waking him up so early after our horrific road trip, but I had to, it was an emergency. He swung his legs over the side of the bed, yawned, and said with sleepy eyes.

"What are you talking about? Dogs swim!"

"Not this dog, he went straight to the bottom. Hurry, we've got to save him!"

132

Dad wrapped his bathrobe around himself and put on his slippers. We headed out, jogging to the spot.

"Here! It was right here! He fell off that rock and he never came up! Jump in and save him, Dad!"

Dad laughed, "That wasn't a dog. It was a seal!"

"It had whiskers, Dad!"

"So do seals," Dad replied.

Then, we heard a lot of barking at a distance.

"Hear them, Dad? It's a bunch of dogs barking."

"Look over to that island, see them—they're seals!"

We headed back to the cottage. "I'm glad you didn't have to jump in that really cold water, Dad."

"Me, too! I'll bet you're starving."

"I'm ready to have a stack of flapjacks, but I'll bet the ones here are not as good as yours, Dad."

After Mom woke up, the three of us headed for the dining hall building, several hundred feet up the long hill. I was starving, after not eating the previous day, eager to have breakfast. In the large dining room, we were guided to our table by the maitre d' and handed a fancy menu.

"This is so lovely," Mom said. "A true vacation for me, not having to cook meals."

Dad had a surprised expression on his face. He whispered to Mom," Don't turn and look in back of you; but you have two famous movie stars sitting behind you, Gary Merrell and Betty Davis."

Mom, surprised, with a big grin on her face, dropped her napkin and took a peek. "You're right! Maybe, I could go over and say hello!"

"No, that would not be a good idea. Movie stars like their privacy," Dad said.

After they jibber-jabbered about the movie stars, a waiter, a young college student on summer break according to Dad, took Mom's breakfast order. Then he walked over to me, holding his pad and pencil. "What may I get for you, young man?"

Starving after a day without food, I said, "I'll take this, this, that...."

"You mind repeating all that, I might have missed an item," he said.

It was the next day when Dad suggested that the two of us go over to the clubhouse to have some fun. Dad and Mom had checked it out the night before, after their dinner. I sprinted up the hill for the building; Dad huffed and puffed up the hill trying to catch up to me. I got there much sooner, ran through the door, and grabbed a long pool stick hanging from the wall. I placed it down on the table with the dark green felt cloth, ready to slam the black 8 ball.

Out of breath, Dad hastily walked through the door and saw me at the pool table ready to take a shot. He waved his hands and yelled with an out of breath voice, "Wait! Don't shoot! You'll rip the felt!"

With the pool table nixed, Dad suggested that we play table tennis. For whatever reason, I wasn't good at any sport I tried. Ping-Pong™ proved to be trickier than I thought it would be. We started out very slow, I was sort of getting a feel for the action. There happened to be a telephone booth close to where Dad was standing. A guy was in there talking on the phone with the booth door open. I guess he did that because it was a stifling hot August day, with awful humidity. Some other kids were playing pinball with lights flashing, bells ringing and other kids playing a board game making a racket, as well. I looked over at the poor guy in the booth. He had to put one finger in his ear to hear whoever he was talking to.

Feeling this was a game I might be good at, I wanted to beat my father. I hit the little white ball with all my might. It sailed through the air with a lot of speed. Dad made an attempt to swing at it but missed, as it shot over his shoulder.

Dad turned and saw that I hit the guy in the booth. Embarrassed and pissed at me, he said, "Why did you do that? You just clobbered Gary Merrell!"

"Well Dad, you're supposed to hit the ball—don't blame me!"

Mr. Merrell put the phone down, rubbed his head, and exited the booth, heading over to me. I thought he might slug me, or at the very least, yell at me.

"Good shot!" he said on his way over, with a smile on his face, as he extended his hand to shake mine.

My Dad, feeling guilty, apologized, "Sorry, he's just learning. Trying to beat his pop. My name is Walt, this is my son. Greg."

"Gary Merrell, here. Pleased to meet you both—it's only my agent—no big deal."

"Sorry, Mr. Merrell, I was just trying to beat my dad and he missed returning the ball."

"Yeah, sorry about that, Gary. We'll be more careful."

"Don't give it a second thought! Have fun!"

On the way back, walking down the hill, I said, "Dad, does that make me famous that I clobbered a movie star? Do you think it will make the papers?"

"No it won't, but it will make a good story to tell all your life."

Arriving at the cottage, I asked my dad if we could fire the handgun. He got it out and we both read the instructions, put the safety on, filled the gun with .22 caliber pellets, and installed the CO_2 cartridge. We took it outside, both standing in front of the railing on the small deck area with four deck chairs. I took the safety off, but before I squeezed the trigger, I looked around.

"What are you looking for," Dad asked.

"Just making sure Mr. Merrell or any other movie stars aren't around." I aimed, and pulled the trigger—Puff! "It fires just like a real gun with a silencer, Dad!"

I took several more shots, my heart racing on each pull of the trigger. Dad took a few shots, too. It was a great father and son moment, one that I would never forget.

So that's how I met Mr. Merrell, learned seals had whiskers, and enjoyed firing my handgun. Oh, one more thing, I added Ping-Pong™ to my list of sports failures.

Chapter 14

Hilltop Church

and the

Whale of a Tale

Mendham Borough, NJ 1942-56

Shortly after I was born in 1942, my parents bought the beautiful white colonial house at 14 East Main Street in Mendham. After they closed on the home, moved in and got settled, Mom, Dad, and I, as an infant, attended our new church home, Hilltop Presbyterian Church. The historic church sat on the hill overlooking the center of town. This would be the church where my family would worship on Sunday mornings while we resided in Mendham. I spent my first years there in the church's nursery while they attended the morning worship service.

Our church leaders had to be inventive where to put all the kids that attended the church's Christian Education Program, including the babies in the nursery. Sunday was a holy day back when I was a kid. All the stores were closed; you couldn't buy gasoline or even an ice cream cone. Kids' sports team activities weren't scheduled on Sundays, either. This may have influenced why so many kids attended Sunday school.

Pastor Philips, church elders, and the teaching staff had done a spectacular job putting together a comprehensive Christian education program at all levels. The parents that volunteered to be teachers spent countless hours reviewing their lesson curriculum and teaching that in their assigned classes. Since Sunday school time coincided with worship time, teachers missed out in attending the church worship service, as well.

Younger children that had mastered how to use crayons in primary level classes were given outlined Bible scenes to color at home. I always looked forward to doing that, even though I didn't do a very good job of coloring within the lines. For whatever reason, being mischievous in Mendham started out early in my life, even before I knew what the word mischievous meant.

It all started one night when I got the brilliant idea to color my table lamp bulb red. I removed the shade and got out a red crayon placing it against the hot bulb. I was amazed at how it melted and got gooey. When I removed it off the bulb, I enjoyed letting my fingers form it into something else, like a tiny coin, ball or just a waxed blob. It didn't take too long before my entire box of crayons got melted down into useless pieces, leaving not one to color with.

My first memorable Sunday school lesson was when I was five, learning about Jonah and the whale. I sat in a small oak chair, along with other kids, listening to our teacher explain the story in a simplistic manner that we would understand.

When our teacher said, with a rousing voice, "The whale swallowed Jonah whole!"

I was terrified and couldn't believe that happened to poor Jonah. The girls sat in horror with tears in their eyes ready to stream down their faces. Before the teacher got a chance to read the second sentence, I blurted out, "How did he see down there in the whale's belly?" This made the situation for Jonah more graphic, causing all the girls to break out crying. It took the teacher forever to comfort each child before she could continue with the story.

She ignored my serious question and continued reading the story. Finally, she read the line in the story, "And the whale spit Jonah out!" Even though Jonah was safe in the end, I'm sure each parent heard about it later that morning, blow by blow. The story was shocking to me too, one that I still remember vividly.

When my parents picked me up from Sunday school, I couldn't wait to tell them about Jonah. My dad was an extravert and liked to talk; my mom was at the other end of the scale— quiet and reserved. As Mom held my hand and we walked out of the church, I desperately tried to retell the story. However, every time I opened my mouth, Dad had run into a church friend to start a new conversation. The story in my head was so fascinating that my brain was going to explode if I didn't get it out soon!

We got in the car and Dad turned the key to head home. The Jonah story had run around inside my little head for the last fifteen minutes, as a vinyl record stuck on one track, getting worse each time around. After Dad paused, saying something to Mom, the story exploded out of my mouth in an alarming way, "Did you know that Jonah got swallowed by a whale in the Bible? That big whale didn't chew him up, either—he just spit Jonah out, flying in the air! Without a bite mark, either, Mom! Do you think the whales at our seashore would do that, Dad?"

Surprised by my question, Dad had a grin on his face, like he wanted to laugh, but knew he shouldn't.

Noticing that, before he could answer, I said, "Dad, this isn't a funny matter, it's not funny at all! Can you imagine if that was you, instead of Jonah, down there in the whale's dark belly?"

Never short on words of wisdom, Dad said, "Son, the whale spit him out before he even knew he got down there."

"So, Jonah was floating around in the whale's mouth, with all those huge teeth? That's even worse!" That night, after I was deep asleep, the story rose up in my head, but worse as an awful nightmare. *It was me going down in whale's belly instead of Jonah. The whale swallowed me and I was trapped inside the whale, searching for a way out. I was on my hands and knees, trying to crawl up and out his slimy belly. I almost got up to his mouth when the stupid whale decided to shoot up to the surface and I slid all the way back down. Then, I got into this long tunnel, a zillion feet long, and I came out of the whale's back end like a rocket!*

I was finally free, doing the doggie paddle, running out of air. I didn't know which way was up when the whale swallowed me a second time." I suddenly woke up, felt my sweaty pillow and blanket, and couldn't believe I wasn't inside the whale. As tears flowed from my eyes like a waterfall, I ran in the darkness to wake my mother to tell her about my horrible dream.

The following year, the stories got better at Sunday school, like when Jesus cured the blind man and brought Lazarus back to life. That was a good thing because I didn't want any more nightmares.

Hilltop did a fabulous job and spent a lot of money for their children's education program. Each student in the upper classes received their own hardbound textbook. To make these special, they contained colored pictures to depict Bible stories. After our lesson was over, we were assigned homework to read the next chapter. I was pretty faithful doing that, except when I got older with too many distractions—experimenting with radio and other stuff, like looking for Granddaddy, that got loose in our house. I ended up speed-reading the chapter fifteen minutes before we left for church.

None of the boys and I liked to practice hymns and struggled to sing them. It didn't help that our voices had all changed. Sometimes when we got bored, we got inventive and changed some of the words in the hymn. It backfired on us at Christmas time when we had to learn hymns to sing at the Christmas Pageant. It all started when one kid got tired of practicing the *We Three Kings* hymn. It was the most important one to memorize, since we would be singing it going down the church aisle at the beginning of the service. Barry came up with some funny words that went like this, "We three king of orient are, trying to smoke a loaded cigar." These words, for whatever reason, got stuck in our heads. That triumphal Christmas Pageant service began with the girls going down the church aisle first, singing the words to *We Three Kings,* flawlessly and the bunch of us staggered along singing our words, "We three kings of orient are, trying to smoke a loaded cigar."

140

Those words are still stuck in my brain and I crack a smile every Christmas when they select that hymn to sing, especially when it gets to that part. So, if you ever sit next to me at church, at Christmas time, and I slip singing, 'loaded cigar,' blame Barry!

This was a neat part about attending Sunday school at Hilltop. In June, a special Sunday was set aside to thank teachers for their service and children for their attendance. Children that attended Sunday school for the year received impressive gold pins to wear. The initial pin was a disk with an engraving on it, about an inch in diameter. It held the additional bars for following years of attendance. If you had perfect attendance, you got an additional award pin. I looked forward to receiving them and wore them proudly each Sunday. After several years of awards, I looked like a three-star general in the military with all the decorative bars and pins on my chest.

In the lower grades, in June, when classes ended, I looked forward to the summer break, more time to play and explore. When the month of July approached, Mom told me that I had to attend Vacation Bible School at Hilltop Church. This was a one-week program. My mom was one of the volunteers that organized the program and taught each summer. In doing that, there was no chance of me not attending.

Even though none of the kids really wanted to go, the teachers did a great job planning the event. We had to read the Bible, sing a few hymns, even the funny one about a Kookaburra bird sitting in the old gum tree. Each year, we were asked to memorize verses in the Bible, something that I wasn't good at. Mid-way through the day, we had juice and cookies. They always came up with a project for us to do, to keep us busy and entertained. One I remember was performing a play, based on a Bible story. Since Jesus, the king of the Jews, was the lead character in the play, they needed a boy for that part.

Mrs. Lane, our teacher, first asked us who would like to play the leading role of Jesus—no one volunteered. She looked around the room from kid to kid, then focused on me.

I swallowed hard, and couldn't believe my bad luck and why, in her right mind, she would pick me.

"Greg, how about you? I think you would be perfect for playing Jesus."

Being a shy kid, I said, "No way, Mrs. Lane! I can't play Jesus, I'm mischievous, not at all like Jesus. Besides, I don't even look like Jesus! Look at my crew-cut, did Jesus have hair like mine?" After my excuse, the other boys came up with some inventive ones, too. I ended up working backstage with lots of other helpers! She came to her senses and selected someone else—a girl.

One year, my mother convinced Al and Sam's mother that it would be a wonderful experience for them to attend Vacation Bible School. That didn't go over well with them. They didn't attend Sunday school, like me, so singing hymns and praying were a new experience for them. The first day, after the session ended, we walked home together. Sam, with a good sense of humor, would start singing a hymn he learned, substituting funny words. He kept us entertained as we laughed all the way.

For seventh and eighth-grade classes, the church ran out of room for older children and rented additional space at the Phoenix House, in the center of town, not far from the church. This was another historic building; it housed the town hall, municipal offices, courtroom, and now some of Hilltop's Sunday School classrooms.

In September, I headed for the Phoenix House, along with twenty other kids. We gathered in a large room filled with rows of folding chairs with hymnals placed on each seat. An older lectern with lots of dents and scratches stood in front of the chairs. Standing behind the lectern was an anxious man, our leader, dressed in a formal suit and yellow striped tie, ready to begin. He shifted his feet, glanced several times at his wristwatch, then checked the open doorway for any latecomers.

Most of the girls filled the room with chatter and giggles, while the boys sat uneasily, shifting positions on their chairs, wishing they were somewhere else.

"Good morning and welcome to an exciting year of seventh and eighth-grade Sunday school," our leader said with a smile.

Dave looked at me; he rolled his eyes and turned both hands palm side up, failing to see any possibility of excitement.

He asked us to stand and turn to page 223 and sing verses 1, 3 and 5. There was no piano in the room, so we had to sing in acapella. During the first stanza, the only voices heard were from the sopranos and our leader. Since I was Greg one note, I mouthed the hymns in silence, holding the book in front of my face. My singing voice had gone south, out of harmony, for whatever reason. After we sang the hymn and prayed, the leader segregated the girls to go to one classroom room and us to another, down the hall.

Our group, including myself, really didn't want to be there. For me, I'd rather be home listening to shortwave or building a radio. For the other boys, they would rather be tossing a ball or playing outside with their friends.

I shuffled my feet in a slow gait to get to our classroom with the rest of the kids, anxiously waiting for the Sunday school session to end. We walked into our room. At the head of the wooden table was our teacher with a stack of textbooks, a pitcher of juice, and a plate filled with jelly donuts, with some filling oozing out. He wore a black suit and red tie, looked to be about forty, and wore a pleasant smile, somewhat hidden by his black mustache. He looked a lot like Tom Selleck does today starring on *Blue Bloods*, on TV. We all sat down on the folding chairs, looking somewhat tense, a bit nervous, not knowing what he expected of us in class. He gestured a warm welcome with open hands and said:

"Good morning, my name is Mr. Johnson; I'm your new teacher. I want to welcome you here this morning."

He chuckled with a grin and said, "I know this is painful for you to be here, you'd rather be home sleeping-in or having fun doing something else. But, let's make the best of this. We have a lesson plan to follow using these textbooks, one for each of you. Let's get to work, do what we need to do and whatever time we have left, we'll talk about anything you like to talk about while munching on these fresh bakery jelly donuts and juice."

The thought, *"Now that's the kind of teacher I like,"* went through my head.

We took turns reading the first chapter in our new books, did that at lightning speed, and answered all the questions at the end of the chapter. We each closed our books with a slam, grabbed a jelly donut, taking a large bite, as jelly oozed out of some, leaving a ring of powdered sugar around our lips. It would have made quite a picture with white rings on each of our mouths. He was a great guy to have as a teacher. He always remembered to bring snacks and joined us in conversation to shoot the breeze on whatever subject we brought up to talk about.

As a growing skinny boy, by the pencil marks on the kitchen door jam, jumping inches each year, I couldn't get enough food. I ate at least two helpings at dinnertime, sometimes three—not feeling so great after the third! Hilltop had a great social event every month, one that I looked forward to attending. There would be two, eight-foot tables, loaded with delicious food items; casserole of meatballs, barbequed spare-ribs, hamburgers, stew, oven-baked beans topped with bacon, salads, rolls, and many other delicious things. Most moms were homemakers when I was a kid. They had lots of time coming up with great recipes to bring to this event each month.

Approaching the church for Friday night potluck suppers, I could smell the wonderful aromas wafting up from the kitchen basement, especially as I entered the church. The potluck suppers were well attended and my parents never had to twist my arm to go. After the two tables were arranged with food, we sat down and waited for Pastor Philips to say the blessing.

As he finished with an, "Amen," I darted to get in line, leaving my parents in the dust, with a plate in my hand, waiting to be filled to the brim for helping number one.

Decades later, as an adult, I met up with one of my former grade school classmates. When we were in conversation one day, he mentioned that he went to Hilltop Church. A big question came to my mind, since I remembered that he went to another church.

"Todd, I remember you and your family attending the United Methodist Church on East Main Street."

He chuckled and said, "I attended whatever church had the best food!"

The big food event at Hilltop was the yearly turkey dinner that was as a fundraiser for the church. It was a town event. No matter what church you attended, everyone looked forward to it. It was so popular they had to limit the number of people attending. They did this by selling so many tickets and there was always a rush for them. It was like trying to get tickets to see the *Avengers: End Game* movie today! You also had to select a dinner serving time. This prevented an overwhelming number of people arriving all at once. It took many church members to make the event possible. They even used the youth to collect tickets, seat families, and return dirty dishes to the basement from the dining area on the first floor.

To run food up to the first floor and dirty dishes back down to the basement, kitchen workers, including me, used a dumbwaiter. You placed whatever needed to be moved into the dumbwaiter, then used the attached rope to raise or lower what was loaded inside.

Loving mechanical and electronic things, I was mesmerized with the dumbwaiter. In my younger years at the church, a thought raced in my mind, to get inside it and play elevator man.

Later, when I was a teen in eighth-grade, my parents approached the board of deacons about gifting an electronic chime system to Hilltop Church.

145

My father obtained a quote from Allied Radio for a system that would do this. A couple of months later, the Hilltop Church Deacons approved their gift. After the Mendham town officials put their stamp of approval on the project, Dad placed the order. Several weeks later, Railway Express delivered it to our home.

As a teenager fascinated with electronics, I couldn't wait to open the boxes. A little voice inside my head said: *Better wait until Dad gets home.* When four o'clock rolled around, I sat on one of the large boxes and waited for Dad to pull into the driveway—minutes turned into hours. Dad's Chevy Nomad station wagon pulled into the driveway. When he stopped the car and got out, he walked over to the stack of boxes.

"Hey, Dad! They're here! Can I open the boxes to look at the equipment?"

"Let's keep it together in the box, this way, nothing will get lost. Saturday, you and your brother-in-law, Bert, can install it at the church. I'm sure you know how to hook it up, but read the instructions just the same. I don't want you blowing out any fuses!"

****

Saturday arrived, as Bert and I headed for Hilltop Church with the boxes and his toolbox. Two of the boxes contained the large speakers, technically called a horn, because they were made of metal. The other boxes contained the public address amplifier, record player, and other parts for the installation.

We carried the horns to the balcony where we would gain access to the steeple. In the balcony office, we set up an extension ladder and popped open the ceiling panel. We walked across the ceiling to access the four flights of rickety wooden stairs, built in the 1800s, carrying the heavy horns, cable, and tools. This got us to the where the huge church bell was mounted. Out of breath, we stopped to rest, as wind raced through the ventilating slats making ghostly noises.

146

Damn, there are even ghosts hanging out here in the bell tower, then I thought, *no wonder, with hundreds of dead people buried out there.* After we caught our breath, we worked our way around the bell to the last flight of stairs leading to the top section. Peeking out one of the slat openings, I got a scenic view of Mendham. I peered down on my school, the brook that ran behind it, downtown buildings, and even birds that sat high on the top of trees.

After our breathtaking view of Mendham, we got to work. Back then, there were no battery-operated tools, so we had to use a hand drill, and wrench to lag bolt the heavy horns to structural wooden beams. I wired the cables while Bert routed the other ends of the cables to a clothes closet down five flights of stairs to the church balcony. Finished, I bagged my tools and started exploring around up there, something I always liked to do. I had placed my right hand into a void of space near the outside wall and felt something smooth and sort of round. *What in the world is it?* I carefully grabbed it and pulled it out.

I sat in disbelief on what I had found, an original Edison filament light bulb. (Edison was an inventor that patented the device in his New Jersey West Orange Laboratory. He obtained patents in 1878 and 1879 on the design. In 1880 the Edison light Company began commercially manufacturing the bulbs.) This was one of those—a piece of history! My heart raced as I thought about the famous inventor and having found one of his bulbs—maybe one he made himself! To keep it safe, I removed my undershirt and wrapped the bulb in it and placed it on top of my tool bag carrying it down to the bell area. I no sooner got there, when an unexpected wind gust knocked me against the bell, resulting in a loud gong that startled me. *Maybe the ghosts were protecting this bulb, hoping to turn it on someday.*

Supporting myself, I carefully got up and exited down the small floor opening, walking backward down all four flights of stairs, because there were no handrails to hold on to. Reaching the balcony, I came down through the ceiling access.

"Bert! You'll never guess what I found! An Edison light bulb!"

He carefully took it from me and wiped the decades of dust off it.

"You're absolutely right! What a find!"

****

The following Sunday, I arrived twenty minutes before church started and headed for the balcony closet. I turned on the amplifier watching the vacuum tubes light up through the ventilation slots. I placed the chime vinyl record on the player and set the arm gently on the record. I turned the volume up when the first chime rang out echoing throughout the church. I hurried down the stairs, and out the door to the front lawn to admire the beautiful hymn that was being chimed out all over town.

Pastor Philips came outside, too. He headed in my direction and said, "Well done! Sounds great!"

****

For many years, church deacons took turns running the system that welcomed worshipers each Sunday. When I recently rejoined the church, years later, the chime system no longer existed, but I could still hear the chimed hymns in my memory.

Chapter 15

We May Have Sounded Flat,

But We Thought We Were Sharp!

Mendham Borough, NJ 1950-1956

I was in fourth-grade, along with my fellow classmates, when Mrs. Clooney opened her desk drawer and pulled out a black colored flute. She stood in front of the class and played *London Bridge Is Falling Down.*

Tommy, sitting in front of me, turned around and said, "Did you know Mrs. Clooney played the flute?"

"No idea! I didn't know anyone else in this room played anything except, *Chop Sticks,* on their grandmother's piano," I replied.

After she finished playing it, she walked around the classroom to show us the musical instrument and said to us, "This is called a song flute that you'll learn how to play soon. Over the next few months, you'll learn how to read music, learning the notes, and timing." She set it down on her desk and picked up a stack of papers and continued, "Take one of these mimeographed forms and pass them on to your neighbor so that everyone has one. Take it home and have your parents place four-dollars in an envelope with your name on it, to purchase your song flute and music book."

After Tommy grabbed his copy, he passed the rest to me and started sniffing his form.

I whispered to him, "Tommy, what are you doing?"

"My brother told me if you inhale this stuff it'll make you feel really good like you're a little drunk because that smelly stuff is alcohol."

"I'm glad you're enjoying it! It may make you feel good, but it makes me nervous and sick to my stomach when I get a whiff of that stuff. Whenever I smell that, I know a test is coming, especially when I go by the mimeograph room with Mrs. Clooney in front of the machine going clickety-click-click."

"My brother must be crazy. I'm not feeling good at all, I feel like I'm ready to barf!" Tommy said, looking at me with a scrunched up face like he was ready to puke.

"You look bad, really bad."

****

Three weeks later, on a Monday, we arrived in our classroom with something on the blackboard that I had never seen before, five white lines going sideways and a funny looking swiggle thing on the left side of the lines. After the bell rang, we stood facing the flag, placed our hand over our heart, and said *The Pledge of Allegiance*. When we sat back down in our seats, Mrs. Clooney handed out our song flutes. They were packaged in cardboard boxes. She went back to her desk and got the stack of music books to pass out to us.

In a flash, everyone opened their box, tearing the flaps off to get at their song flute, as if it was a long-awaited birthday present. Soon, we all had them in our mouths blowing out every note the instrument could play. This sounded like spooky movie background music. When I blew mine twice, it sounded like a steam train whistle—woo woo!

Jerry, sitting across from me, tapped me on the shoulder and said, "You sound like my Lionel™ train set at home!"

The notes continued to fill the room with noise rather than any sort of melody.

"Okay! That's enough! Put them down," Mrs. Clooney said in a stern manner.

Through the weeks we were taught to play the instrument using our music books.

We learned what hole on the flute we had to cover to sound the notes: C, D, E, F, G, A, and B. Along with the notes, we were taught timing, how long to blow to get quarter, half, and whole notes. When we practiced, we had to tap our feet so that we would all be in time. Some kids were confused because the musical scale didn't have an H and I as the alphabet did. I confused the rest of the class when I raised my hand.

"How come, Mrs. Clooney, an octave isn't A, B, C, D, E, F, and G?"

"That is how the musical scale was developed, Greg, each octave starts with the note of C."

The first song we learned was *Mary Had a Little Lamb*. It was a proud moment when we all finished the song.

I turned the page in my blue book and said to Jerry, "You'll never guess what the next song is—*London Bridge*! That's a baby song!"

An amazing sound of music filled our classroom that day. We all thought we were sharp musicians but somehow fell flat when some kid played the wrong note. The song flutes were a great way to introduce us to music. I enjoyed mine and so did my classmates.

****

One year later, in fifth-grade, our little black song flutes got stored in a drawer or someplace else at home, maybe for a younger sister or brother. Mine went for better use, rather than get stored in a drawer. I sawed it in three pieces to make insulators for my radio antenna. I was kind of sad when I looked at the three pieces in my hand. *Oh well, so much for the song flute.*

Since we were such maestros at the song flute, my class graduated to all sorts of fancy brass and silver musical instruments. That happened during our first week of school. Our teacher, Mr. Roscoe, directed us to go down to the music room to meet Mr. Arnold, the school's new music teacher.

I walked in the room with the rest of the kids in my class. Mr. Arnold was standing in front of one of the tables that had an arrangement of musical instruments across it. He had long black hair, pulled back in a ponytail, and a waxed mustache coming to points on each side.

Jerry nudged me with his elbow and whispered in my ear, "He looks like a musician with that long hair of his."

"Please sit down," he said.

After we were seated, he said, "Good morning class! My name is Mr. Arnold. I'm proud to be here at your school as your new music teacher. It is a joy for me to have you as my students."

Tommy, sitting next to me, whispered, "He'll eat those words the first week we have those instruments in our hands!"

He placed his hand on one of the horns and said, "Today, I will demonstrate each one of these instruments, playing a few notes to help you decide which one you would like to play."

He started playing the first one, a trumpet.

"That's the one I want to play," I whispered to Tommy. "It reminds me of the ones the cavalry play when they ride off on their horses, charging after the Indians."

"You'd better think about that again. I don't see any horses around here," he giggled under his breath.

The teacher picked up the second instrument with the thing that slides back and forth with each note.

"This is a trombone," he said, playing a short tune.

Joe, on the other side of me, tapped me on the arm and said, "That's going to be the one for me!"

When he grabbed the tuba and sounded a few deep notes, Joe changed his mind and said, "I like that one better, although it does sort of sound like a foghorn."

I sarcastically said, "Good luck on that!"

The last instruments he played were the clarinet and flute. They were the ones that the girls in my class all chose.

After the demonstration, our teacher invited us to do a touchy-feely and try them. Joe headed for the tuba struggling to pick it up, almost hitting Claire in the head with the huge horn. After getting it in place, he put his mouth on the mouthpiece. He might have blown it a little too hard when an unexpected note came blasting out of his backside. Claire gave him a dirty look and moved far away to the other side of the room.

As Joe's face got a bit red. I said to him, "You'd better stick to the trombone! You do that in an orchestra and you'll get kicked out the first performance!"

After everyone tried an instrument and sat back in their chairs, Mr. Arnold passed out a rental agreement form to each of us and asked us to pencil in the instrument we wanted to learn to play. He went around the room and glanced at our choices. He seemed pleased with them as he smiled and said, "I see a great band in the future."

Tommy turned to get our attention and said, "Good luck on that!" he chuckled.

That afternoon I got home from school and handed my form to Mom.

"Oh, you chose the same instrument as your brother, Walter."

"I never saw him play a trumpet, Mom."

"He used to, but gave that up to yodel instead."

"What's yodeling, Mom?"

My mother attempted to demonstrate, yodeling, "Oh lady, oh lady, who!"

I laughed so much that my stomach hurt. After a while, I had to ask her to yodel again because it was just so funny to hear.

"If I give up on the trumpet, there is no way I'll take up yodeling, Mom!"

Later that evening, when Dad came in the door after a long drive out to Long Island and back, looking like he was ready to drop, I said, "Dad, I got some good news for you." Dad looked at me with a 'what now' expression. From experience, he never knew what to expect in my childhood journey, especially after the Granddaddy incident, with a snake slithering throughout the house for two weeks.

"Okay, let's have it."

"I'm going to learn to play the trumpet!"

He looked at me and said in a serious tone, "Please practice before I get home."

A week later, a truckload of instruments in black leather storage cases got delivered to the borough school. Sam and Al's class got theirs, too. After the 3:15 bell rang, I walked home with them. Halfway there, Sam couldn't wait any longer. He set down the case, flipped open the clasps and grabbed the horn, playing a string of notes. He definitely had some hidden talent none of us knew about. Al and I left ours in the case, knowing we had a lot of learning and practicing to do before we caught up to Sam.

When I got home, I ran into the house to show Mom my instrument. She was as excited as I was, as I opened the case. I grabbed the trumpet and played a couple of notes.

"I know you'll do well. When you set your mind to do something you accomplish it," she said.

I went to my room and placed the trumpet on my bed to do my homework. It was about five when I picked up the horn and started blowing some notes using the three buttons and combinations of them. I had been playing for about a half-hour when I heard a knock on my door.

"Yes?" I asked.

"Can you give that thing a drink," Dad said. "I've got one doozy of a headache and every time you blow that trumpet, it's like a spike being hammered into my brain. I'm going to take some aspirin and lay down."

I put the brain killer back in the case to bring back to school the next day when the town's fire siren started going off. This was unfortunate with Dad's awful headache. The siren was located close to our house, only a block away, high on a telephone pole. There was no problem hearing it at our house, for sure. Things even vibrated inside our house when it went off. The siren continued, and seemed to go on forever, going off to first signal the street and then the house number. When I thought it had ended it began again to repeat the information, to make sure the firefighters went to the right house. The guy on the siren button must have considered that, as he repeated the signal for the third time.

"Jee's, what's the whole town burning down?" Dad shouted from his bedroom. "Why can't the firemen just follow the fire trucks?" Dad asked, as Mom went for an ice pack.

The next day, Dad felt better but looked kind of pale. Mom said to me that he might have had a particular type of headache, "A mindgrade." A new word for me, I would have to look that up in the dictionary. I felt guilty because I probably caused his mindgrade and thought, *I'm even mischievous playing the trumpet.*

The weeks went by. I practiced the trumpet almost every day, making sure Dad was not home. After weeks of that, I got tired of blowing the horn after it started to give me a headache. So I brought it back to school to be returned to the rental company along with a signed note from my mother. When I stepped into the music room, I held the case and handed the note to Mr. Arnold.

After reading it, he suggested, "How about playing the flute?"

"Well, the last one I had, I sawed into three pieces!"

155

His smile changed into a look of horror when he heard that. I handed him the case and said, "Here you are, Mr. Arnold. I don't want to play this thing anymore. It's giving everyone around the house a mindgrade, including me!" He quickly walked away to lock the instrument in a storage area.

Chapter 16

My Sidekick Steve,

The Bees, a Cow's Teats,

and the 300 lb. Mower

Mendham Borough, NJ 1955-1957

I was a mid-forties surprise for my mother—she and my dad didn't plan it that way. They thought that their family had been completed. Then Mom noticed some anatomical changes in her body. I'm sure that bump was an anxious time for both of them. They had no idea how anxious, until years later when I held a soldering iron in my hand building electronic stuff. Coming into the world would mean that I would have a sister twenty years older and a brother twelve years older. With the tremendous age difference between my siblings, I couldn't play with either, but luckily I had a wonderful nephew, Stephen, five years younger. He, my sister Wilma, and her husband, Bert, lived next door to us. Steve and I were best buddies, he was more like a younger brother than a nephew.

(Steve) - Stephen D. Fischer

****

Steve palled around with me, interested in the stuff my friends, Al, Sam, and I were doing. Often, we played together. He watched with fascination as we built experimental radios or something else. It got more exciting for him when we went to test it, plugging it into an electrical outlet to see if it worked.

At times it got interesting when it started buzzing, our hopes high that it worked, then suddenly burst on fire. When things went awfully wrong, I blew a fuse putting several areas of the house without power, including my Mom's favorite radio show, *Arthur Godfrey*. We had some great childhood experiences together and unfortunately some painful ones, too, that we still talk about as adults.

One time, when I was thirteen and Steve eight, the two of us, on a sunny spring day, decided to plant our very own vegetable garden, a victory garden. There was a food shortage, long after World War II, and the government asked everyone that had land to help out by growing gardens. We were going to help our country and be patriotic. There just happened to be an empty plot of land near the infamous haunted red barn, about fifty by fifty feet, that we thought would make an excellent spot for a garden.

So we got a pitchfork out of the tool shed, went to the plot of ground, and started to turn the soil over. Being older and stronger, I started the arduous task of turning over the dirt. It was hard work, jamming the tines into the earth and lifting up the dirt and flipping it over. Steve watched patiently as I worked preparing the soil. As blisters formed on my hand, I needed to take a break.

"Want to give it a try, Steve?"

Steve was eager to give it a go after standing there watching me dig for a half an hour. He said, "Sure."

He stuck the fork into the ground and went to turn it over, when hundreds of angry yellow jackets came flying out after us. Steve got stung the worst, as the bees immediately climbed up his pant legs stinging him multiple times. We tried to scare them away by swatting at them, but that made them angrier. We ran for our lives, yelling at the top of our lungs, "Help! Help!" We ran looking for a safe place to escape the bees.

"Over there—the police car!" I screamed.

Mendham's police car was sitting in the driveway, about a hundred feet away. Fortunately, it was unlocked and we both piled into the front seat. The Mendham Police stencil on the side door didn't deter the bees at all, as hundreds of bees followed us inside, stinging us. Stung severely, we jumped out the opposite door, hoping the bees wouldn't follow, but they did.

"Run to your house!" I yelled to Steve. We split for our homes, running as fast as we could, screaming all the way. At home, our mothers tweezed out all the stingers and soothed the areas with witch hazel. Needless to say, that ended our bright idea of being patriotic and having a victory garden for the foreseeable future if bees lurked in the ground—our country would be short our contribution.

****

Feeling sorry for our garden failure, Steve's folks invited me to join them the following weekend, to visit the Sussex County Fair. Neither Steve nor I had ever gone to a fair before. We all piled into their car and made the trek to the fair. When we got there, we parked on a grass field with hundreds of other cars. We walked a distance to the entrance, paid our admission, and went through the gate, overwhelmed with things to see. No matter where you looked, there were farm animals. They were beautiful to look at, not like the ones on farms in Mendham. These owners brushed and groomed their animals to make them look like household pets. Some had already been judged with colored ribbons dangling proudly from their necks.

We especially loved the demonstration on how to milk a cow. A teenage girl, dressed in a bright red and white plaid shirt, wearing a pair of farmers' jeans, was busy at work doing something under her cow as milk rhythmically squirted into the pail. We couldn't quite see what kind of magic she was doing with her hands to make the milk come out.

"Do you think she tickles the cow's belly to get milk?" Steve asked.

160

"Steve, we've got to get closer to see what she's doing under that cow," I said. We moved up, really close, so close that I could smell the fragrance of her perfume waft under my nose.

She felt our presence, turned, looked at me, and asked with a big smile, "Do you want to try it?"

"Me?" I asked with apprehension, pointing my finger at my chest.

"Yeah, you. You look like you have a little bit of kid farmer in you. You've got to wash your hands first, though. There's some soap and water over there in the other pail and a towel to dry them off."

I headed for the pail and wondered what I got myself into. After I washed, she was waiting for me to share this special experience.

"Okay, that's good. Sit on the stool with your legs open, so you can get at her utter," she said.

"Her utter?" I said, a bit alarmed. I sat down, turned, and looked at Steve wearing a smile, ready to break out laughing any minute.

"Grab her teats," she said, cracking a smile.

"You better show me how—I've never touched these things before." I looked at the things hanging down and asked, "Are they teats or tits—I always get those two mixed up, which is which?" She looked a bit puzzled, then looked me in the eye and said, "Teats. Cows have teats." She pointed to the things hanging down.

Confused, I asked, "Which ones? There's so many."

"Take your pick," she said.

As I wrapped my fingers around the two closest teats; they felt soft and warm like holding two giant worms.

161

"Now, squeeze and pull down one," she said. "That's good, now squeeze and pull down with the other hand, and keep the rhythm going back and forth."

I watched as milk squirted into the pail with every squeeze. Thrilled with my success, my chest proudly expanded and I could feel my smile growing with every squeeze. I must have been doing a great job—several families walked over to watch.

"See how well you're doing it? You're a real natural. You'd make a great milk farmer," she said.

"I would?" Then I turned to Steve, "Hey buddy, if I fail at electronics, blowing things up, I could always be a dairy farmer doing this all day long!"

"Careful, you're squirting out of the pail," the girl warned.

I turned back, continuing the process, happy as a lark, singing the tune from *Green Acres*. "Green Acres is the place for me...." I could hear the kids who stood with their parents, laughing their heads off when I began to sing.

From some distance away, Wilma said, "Okay, Greg. You played dairy farmer long enough, let's move on to see the rest of the fair."

"Okay, sis." I got up off the stool and said to the teenage girl, "Thanks for letting me milk your cow. I can't wait to tell my buddies."

Pointing to the underside of the cow, she whispered into my ear, "Remember, these are called teats, not tits. I wouldn't want you to get me or you in trouble."

I whispered back to her, "I forget a lot of stuff, but I'll be sure to remember something as important as teats and tits all my life. If I ever slipped and told my mother that I pulled a couple of tits at the Sussex County Fair, she'd wash my mouth out with Ivory soap™ and ground me for a least a month!"

"That doesn't sound pleasant," she replied.

162

"It's the worst! Believe me! It's happened a couple of times."

"Let's go look at the horses," My sister, Wilma, shouted above the din of the crowd.

I sprinted up to my sister and said, "I'm staying clear of those things—horses and I don't have a good history. Whenever I get near them, something crazy happens!"

"We'll watch the rodeo barrel races instead," she suggested.

Steve and his parents stood against the fence, while I watched from a safe distance as each horse zoomed around the course.

After the race, we enjoyed some great tasting hotdogs and walked away with cotton candy sticks in our hands. Later in the afternoon, a tractor pulling contest was going to take place.

"We've got to see that tractor pulling contest," Steve said.

One hour later, we stood behind a fence and watched as huge farm tractors pulled heavily weighted sleds from a dead-start. We both loved tractors, and we were glued to the action.

I whispered to Steve, "We've got to try that with our fathers' tractors."

"That would be a blast," he responded.

The following Monday, after school, I went over to Steve's house to play. I saw him pulling a red wagon around his backyard and headed over to talk to him.

He said with excitement, "That tractor pull we saw yesterday was amazing!"

"Yeah, I really enjoyed that. Too bad we couldn't have a pull with my dad's big Farmall tractor."

"You're not old enough to drive that," Steve reminded me.

"I got news for you. I started it up, put it in first gear, and landed outside the barn. I'm thankful that I didn't have it in reverse and go right through the barn."

163

We both chuckled over that thought and how my father would respond to a hole in the barn in the form of a tractor with a kid sitting on it.

"We could have a tractor pull with our dads' walk-behind tractors, just like we talked about at the fair," Steve suggested.

"That would be fun—let's do it! We'll call it, The Mendham Fair tractor pull!"

Steve's dad had a David Bradley™ tractor with large diameter tires, almost a yard tall. My dad had a much smaller Bollens™ tractor with tires about two feet in diameter. I went to the red barn, started my dad's tractor and headed for Steve's yard with a length of steel chain over my shoulder. Arriving there, I backed my tractor up to the David Bradley.

"Let's chain them together," I said.

"My end is ready," Steve said with a grin.

I fastened my end, and said, "Let see who wins!"

Each of us pushed our tractor's throttle to the max. Both engines screamed as gray smoke shot out of both exhausts.

"Ready, Steve? Put it in gear on the count of three! 1...2...3!"

The chain went taught and all four tractor wheels dug-in, tossing the grass from underneath the wheels into the air. Soon, the wheels dug channels into the lawn as the tire treads continuously threw dirt all over the place. That included us, since we had to hold the handlebars steady, to keep the tractors pulling in a straight-line. We continued to let the tractors battle it out, neither one had gained an inch. The two tractors continued to struggle to try to win. Steve's tractor suddenly stalled, with my tractor pulling his tractor backward, out of the two ruts in the lawn.

"I'm the winner!" I declared, as I shut down the Bollens™. The tractor engines were so hot that I saw heat waves coming off the over-worked engines. Thank goodness, neither tractor suffered any damage.

164

After they cooled down, we drove them back where we got them. Our dads were never the wiser on the abuse the tractors were subjected to.

****

Steve loved machines as much as I did. Inside the red barn was an antique Jacobson estate reel mower. It weighed over hundreds of pounds. It not only cut the grass but rolled the lawn, as well, with heavy solid steel rollers. To lubricate the internal piston inside the motor, it had an oiler that dribbled oil, a drop a minute, into the air intake to lubricate the piston. There were two heavy steel flywheels, one on each side of the motor to give momentum to the driveshaft as the piston fired.

One side had a long shaft that connected to a Bosch™ magneto that generated a super high voltage spark for the spark plug. To start the machine you had to use a large crank, the size you would use to start a Model A Ford™ car with.

My father always warned, "Don't put your thumb around the crank handle. If the motor back-fires, you'll end up with a broken thumb, facing backward."

Steve and I got the brilliant idea of having the heavy-duty estate mower pull the both of us in our red wagons behind the mower, like a train pulling two railway cars. We only had to get it working. It was a bugger to start, sometimes taking an hour or more to accomplish.

The two of us slid the barn door open. We went inside to make sure it was safe, grabbed the heavy machine and struggled to get it outside. I went back in to retrieve my dad's gas can to fuel the mower. The engine's oiler was full, so I flicked it to on, to start dripping oil into the engine.

"Ready?" I asked Steve. I gave the crank a spin——nothing! I continued to turn the crank until my face turned to red and I was out of breath. I couldn't let Steve crank it since it took a lot of strength to turn-it-over. I had all I could do to crank it myself. After I rested, I was still hot and removed my T-shirt to cool down. I was ready to try again.

With my attention focused on the crank handle, I didn't see Steve's hand go to touch the uninsulated spark plug electrical contact while he braced himself with his other hand on my back. I gave the crank a fast turn and got the shock of my life. Steve and I flew backward from the jolt, landing on our butts, both of us dazed. God only knows what our heart rhythms were doing—I'm sure they were erratic as hell.

"You okay, Steve?"

"Besides a pin-hole burn on my finger and feeling kind of dizzy, I'll be okay. You should have told me you were going to crank it—some buddy you are! How about you, are you okay?"

"Are you kidding? I feel like I got clobbered with a bolt of lightning!"

After sitting on the cool ground for a while, we both felt better and tried to start the mower again. I gave it another swift crank. The engine sputtered, then backfired with an alarmingly loud **POW**!

"I hope the police didn't hear that and think we just shot the Larson's cannon off again," I said.

The next crank, it started with a putt, putt, putt. We raced to get our two wagons and rope them together behind the mower. We spent about an hour cruising around our yards with smiles on our faces.

"Wasn't this worth getting knocked on your ass, Steve?"

"Are you kidding? I'll never go near a spark plug for the rest of my life!"

****

Steve continued to pal around watching my buddies and I play around with electronic circuits. A few years after I got my amateur radio license, he got his. Steve's great achievements continued. His interest in electronics grew from playing around with me and my other friends, Al and Sam, as we built stuff together.

After graduating from West Morris Regional High School, Steve continued his education at Worcester Polytechnic Institute (now WPI) in Massachusetts, graduating with a BSEE and enjoyed 13 job offers! He was hired by Hewlett-Packard, a proud achievement for his family, including me.

Chapter 17

Showdown at Lane's Pond

(Follow-up chapter to "The 2nd Amendment" in *Mischievous in Mendham*.)

Mendham Borough, NJ 1957

After my horrific accidental discharge with my twenty-two rifle, lodging a bullet in the second story barn rafter, I immediately removed the firing pin and placed the gun in a safe location—my clothes closet. Thank God it fired into the haunted barn and not into Al, Sam, or myself. Reality hit home after that incident—guns are lethal and not safe for kids, especially us.

****

At 3:15 the bell rang and I headed out of my 7th-grade classroom to walk home with my pals Al and Sam. It was a gorgeous Monday, the last week in May. It was so warm; we carried our light jackets in our hands. We had reached the Sinclair™ Gas Station on Main Street when Sam came up with an idea.

"Let's explore that little brook that starts behind the station," Sam suggested.

"Sound okay to you, Greg?" Al asked.

"Sure! Better than sitting inside driving ourselves nuts trying to invent something," I replied.

Forty-five minutes later, the three of us, wearing boots, the ones with the large ugly black metal buckles, reached the intersection of East Main Street and Orchard Street.

Timing is everything. Just as we were ready to cross the road, Mendham Borough's one and only police car approached us.

It slowed down, then stopped. It was my brother, Walter, the Chief of Police.

He rolled down his window and sort of gave us a visual check out. "What trouble are you guys up to now?"

He had our number, not so much as three goofballs, but kids doing something they shouldn't, now and then. I gave him the pat answer I always gave my Dad. "Nothing." Then told him, "We're going to explore the Passaic Brook, playing Lewis and Clark along with their sidekick, Andy."

"Make sure that's all you do!" he responded. He rolled up his window and hit the gas on the Ford Interceptor™ as the back tires gave a little chirp against the dry pavement.

We crossed the road to the Sinclair™ Gas Station. They not only sold gas but older used cars, sort of antiques. Two black Model A Fords sat parked on the side, one with a FOR SALE, $200 sign. Behind the station, the property sloped down twenty feet at a steep angle. In one area, water flowed out from an underground river that formed a free-running brook. This terrain served as a convenient dumping ground for the gas station, too. They disposed of their unwanted stuff, coal ashes, motor oil, and other unwanted stuff.

We walked past the Model A's and stood at the end of the property looking down the slope. It didn't even look like dirt but instead like an abandoned oil field. It was so contaminated nothing grew there, not even a dandelion nor any other weed.

"You first. You had better slide down over there. It looks a lot cleaner," Al said to his brother, Sam, as I stood there and watched.

"Here goes nothing," Sam said, as he slid down on his butt to the bottom. He stood up, wiped off his pants and said, "Who's next?"

Al and I slid down next, one after the other. Once down there, we faced a dense growth of cat-o'- nine-tails and clusters of tall bushes.

We pushed them away looking for the brook. Sam was leading our expedition with Al following close behind. Sam bent a tall bush over with his foot and forgot his brother was a couple of paces behind. When he released his foot, the main branch sprung back with a vengeance, smacking Al in the face.

"Ow! My eye! Sam! For God's sake! Be more careful, that branch just whacked me in the face!"

"You okay, Al?" I asked.

"Barely. Everything is a blur through this one eye."

We proceeded through the wild growth and found the spring that gushed water to form a free-running brook. We followed the brook, stomping down the wild growth to make a path.

"Watch out for that stuff, that's poison sumac. I brushed up against that stuff last year and itched for two weeks," Al warned.

"Stop! There's the pond! Look at all those snakes sleeping on the rocks," Sam warned.

"They just came out of hibernation and are warming up," I added.

"The pond must belong to whoever owns that house," Sam said.

"That's Mr. Lane's house. He teaches at Morristown High School. Our older brother, Grant, has him for a biology teacher," Al said.

"I hope his family doesn't swim in that snake-infested pond."

"Why don't we help Mr. Lane and kill the snakes," Sam said.

"And how do you propose we do that?" I asked.

"With your rifle," Sam replied.

"That's not going to happen! We nearly had a fatal accident once; thank God a slug didn't end up in one of our skulls. If my father gets wind of my rifle going off our property, it's curtains for me!"

171

"Oh, come on! It would be so much fun!" Sam teased with a big grin on his face.

"He'll never find out," Al said, as he patted me on the back.

"This is going against every good instinct I have for good judgment. Mr. Lane is probably on his way home now. Can you imagine him seeing three kids using his backyard as a firing range, popping off snakes around his pond?" I warned. "It's not worth the risk. What if my brother catches us with the rifle and locks the three of us up in that jail cell at the police station?"

"You're overreacting. We'll do it tomorrow then, right after school, when he's not home," Al suggested.

"And where are we going to get the twenty-twos?" I asked.

"Jerry—as soon as we get out of here. There's no way we're getting up that oily hill. We'll have to sneak through Lane's yard," Al said.

Reaching the sidewalk, we headed for Jerry's house clomping in our boots.

Jerry was a tall kid with blonde hair, built like a football player. He was a year older than us and went to a private school, Morristown Beard. He was a free-spirited kid. He liked to fool around and made you laugh. He lived on East Main Street, across from Rowe's Sheep Farm.

He didn't share the same interest in doing electrical experiments like us, making an X-ray machine or even a pirate radio station, and stuff like that. He just liked to do target practice. Being older than us, he had more common sense. Whenever we had some brain-drain idea, we came to him for advice, to keep us on the straight and narrow road of wisdom. His parents had a lot of trust in him. So much so, that they bought him his very own twenty-two rifle.

Jerry first got interested in archery, but got tired of pulling the string and wanted to pull a trigger instead. His dad made a firing range of stacked bales of hay to make a protective target wall.

Jerry put one of those bull's-eye targets in the center. Beyond the target area were parcels of undeveloped land and his family's old barn. It wouldn't matter if a few bullets hit that, it was falling apart anyway, board by board. If a bullet strayed, it would eventually go into the ground—totally safe.

We approached Jerry's Mom, sitting behind the wheel in their family's car parked in the back driveway. She was supervising Jerry firing his twenty-two. We walked past her, well behind Jerry. She looked puzzled seeing the three of us wearing tall boots on a sunny day. This probably confirmed her suspicions— goofballs, no doubt about it. Jerry acknowledged our arrival with a wave and while we sat on the ground to watch him finish firing several rounds, hitting the target near dead center each time. He opened the chamber to discard his last shell casing, walked over to the car, and gave the rifle to his mom.

We got up and walked over to him. He glanced down at our feet and then back up at us.

"Do you guys know something that I don't?" Jerry said with a chuckle, then pointed to a perfectly clear sky.

"We just got back from an expedition! Like those guys, Lewis and Clark, and needed boots to walk along the brook," Sam explained, seriously, as if it would appear someday in a history book.

"Yeah, right! Don't you guys have anything better to do?" Jerry asked, shaking his head with another chuckle.

"We were exploring the brook that runs behind the Sinclair gas station and ran into a bunch of snakes," Sam answered. "We got scared, and quit. These things were gigantic, Jerry!"

Al, standing behind Sam and wearing a smile, looked at Jerry and spread his hands about a foot apart.

"We're going to have a showdown with those snakes, shoot every single one of them so the Lanes' can swim in their pond. We need some twenty-two ammo, probably longs. Can you help us out?" Sam asked.

"My mothers has hidden my ammo, or let's say, she thinks she has it hidden. I found several boxes of ammo in the kitchen in one of her food canisters. Where in the world are you going to get a gun?" Jerry asked.

"From Greg, the one he made a firing pin for," Al answered, patting me on the back.

"My father's number one rule, never take the gun off our property," I thought with fear running through my veins. Then I repeated out loud to my buddies, "My dad has a rule about taking the rifle off our property."

"What rule did you break putting a slug in his barn roof?" Jerry asked, with a chuckle. "Where's the gun now?"

"Just standing up in the corner of my closet without the firing pin," I answered.

"Stay here. If the coast is clear, I'll bring you a handful of longs from the kitchen." Jerry walked with his nonchalant gate to the house to retrieve some shells.

Several minutes later, he re-appeared with a smile from ear to ear. He handed them to Al, shielding any parental view from the house. Al took the shells and placed them into his right front pocket.

"Be gentle with them, will you? I don't want to hear that you blew off an important part of your anatomy," Jerry said with a contagious laugh.

"That would be some dilemma! Try to explain that to your bride on your wedding night!" I said as the four of us roared with laughter.

The three of us started walking home. By this time, car traffic increased, as people returned from work. We noticed some drivers staring at us; the unbelievable sight of three boys wearing tall boots on a perfectly clear day.

The next day, I walked home from school, past Lane's house. No one seemed to be home.

The driveway was empty.

That meant that Mr. Lane was still at the high school and there was no sign that his wife was around either. After arriving home, I greeted my mom to let her know that I had arrived.

"I'm going to go over to Al and Sam's house. We're going on an expedition over to that small brook behind the Sinclair™ Gas Station."

"How about a rootbeer float?"

"No thanks, it's not worth getting cavities drilled out and getting gassed, Mom. The dentist told me to stay away from candy and sweets."

"Be back by six," Mom said.

"Will do."

Exercising caution, I nervously removed the rifle out of the closet with my arm shaking. Memories of the accident were still fresh in my mind. I retrieved the firing pin out from my secret hiding place, the model sailboat sitting on my shelf. Since Mom was busy in the kitchen, she wouldn't be able to see me carry the gun out of the house and across the backyard to the Larson's house.

With the rifle in one hand and boots in the other, I snuck out the basement back door for my buddies' house. They were waiting for me wearing their boots. I handed Al the rifle while I put on mine.

"Everyone ready?" Al asked.

Sam and I nodded.

East Main Street was quiet at this time in the afternoon. We held the rifle pointed to the ground between us to hide it as best we could. We crossed Main Street and snuck through the side of Lane's property. None of us thought it was a good idea to slide down the slippery embankment with the gun in our hand.

We'd have a hard time explaining a bullet hole in one of the Model A's. Not having a girl with us, we couldn't claim we were playing Bonnie and Clyde. *Maybe on the next expedition, we can get Kirsten to come with us. Lots of luck with that!* I thought.

"Think it's going to work?" Sam asked.

"I have my doubts. Maybe it was a fluke that it went off in the barn," I answered, as I placed a twenty-two-long into the chamber. "Who's going to take the first shot?"

"You are. If your brother comes with the siren blasting, I want you to be holding the gun," Al said, with a smile.

I walked closer to the pond, sneaking up on the biggest snake, all coiled up on the large flat rock. "Looks like one of those poisonous copperheads," I said. I carefully aimed, held my breath, and gently pulled the trigger. The moment I pulled the trigger, the gun fired with a loud **POW** and a **PING!** The snake popped up in the air and fell into the pond.

"What the hell was that 'Ping' sound?" Sam asked.

"Who cares—you nailed him. Food for the snapping turtles," Al said.

"You guys want to take a turn?"

"Let me take one out," Sam requested. With the gun in his hand, he walked closer to the pond. "I'm going for that other big one."

My brain was grinding away. *Where had I heard that ping sound before? The Lone Ranger show!* "SAM! DON'T SHOOT!"

Sam released his finger off the trigger, uncocked the rifle, and removed the shell from the chamber before walking over to us. "Why not?"

"That loud Ping sound, it was the bullet ricocheting back off the rock at us," I warned.

"You hear a siren?" Sam asked.

"Oh crap! It's got to be the police car with your brother behind the wheel," Al said.

"Sam, hide the damn gun in the weeds—let's get out of here," I said with haste.

We needed to avoid going through Lane's property, that would be trespassing. It was a Laurel and Hardy moment, as we tried to climb the slippery hill. We managed to dig our boot toes into the soft oily dirt and using several rocks poking out, we were able to get up the incline to the back of the gas station. After getting up the hill, we walked to the Main Street sidewalk. The police cruiser skidded to a stop as its red and blue lights swirled around on top of the roof.

"You think we robbed a bank!" Sam whispered with a smirk on his face.

My brother got out of the car, slammed the door, and walked over to us. He always had a happy demeanor, but not today. He scowled, just as police officers do when they're ready to slam on the cuffs.

"I thought I told you, I never wanted to hear that cannon go off again!" my brother shouted at us. "I got a call, over Morris County Police Radio, that there was gunfire in this area, called in by two residents."

"It must have been one of these A's that backfired," I said, avoiding looking my brother in the face.

"Backfire, my eye! Don't let me catch you with a gun or that cannon you used on Halloween. I gave the three of you one pass, you won't get another."

The warning sunk in. We walked in silence to the Larson's house, then I split through their back yard to mine. The following day we met after school to get the gun. I was able to return it to my closet without my mother catching me in the act.

It was several weeks later when I went into my closet and noticed that the rifle barrel that had always stuck up had disappeared. I tossed things out of the closet to make sure it wasn't behind something. I only found one rifle.

The one I forgot I still had—the stupid cork gun, the one that killed the bird in my parent's cuckoo clock a few years back on New Year's Eve.

That was the last time I ever saw the twenty-two-rifle. On one or two occasions, Al, Sam, and I went out on an expedition with the cork gun. It wasn't a real rifle, but we pretended it was. We tried shooting a rabbit that was hiding out in the grass one day, but the rabbit just ran away. It may have killed my folks cuckoo, but it certainly couldn't take out a rabbit.

Al and Sam, twins, at an earlier age

Chapter 18

They Blamed the Damn Russians,

But

It Was Me

Barnegat Light, NJ 1957

I was in my freshman year at Morristown High School when June rolled around. It was a time of intense study to review all the material that I had learned over the previous months, since last September. My brain was on overload. After completing final exams, I handed in my textbooks and took a sigh of relief, glad that school was over. The teachers and administration were good, no complaint there. However, the rough group of characters dressed in black leather jackets and the huge class sizes made the school an unpleasant place to attend. It wasn't only my opinion either, other districts were displeased sending their students there, as well. At the time, some of them tried to leave that district but were denied the necessary approval to do so.

Nearing retirement, my parents put their Mendham house on the market and planned to rent an apartment in Morristown. That would mean that I would have to attend three more years at MHS, while my Mendham classmates would attend a brand new high school, West Morris Regional. I was very jealous of them.

I wasn't happy about my parents selling or moving. The only good thing about the summer of 1957 was our vacation for two weeks on Long Beach Island at Barnegat Light. Two of my best friends; Al, Sam, and their sister, Kirsten, were there for the entire summer. She happened to be the mecca of my eye, the most beautiful young woman I had ever seen. I was completely smitten with her, a true princess.

That summer vacation, I also looked forward to doing lots of skin diving with my new equipment and doing some ham radio. I had my beginners Novice Amateur Radio FCC (Federal Communications Commission) License hoping to be able to set up a portable transmitting and receiving station there. All of the radio equipment that I had brought, I had built myself, from junk parts; the stuff people in town put out for the garbage man. The antenna that I used was fabricated from copper wire, unwound from an old power transformer. My station equipment may have been built from junk, but over the past winter months, I had contacted several stations from other states outside of New Jersey. My most treasured contact was one that I had made at midnight all the way to California.

Before I knew it, it was July and we were getting ready to go on vacation. At around nine in the morning, my dad and I were packing the car with our suitcases and a stockpile of food to start the week with. That included a cooler filled with meats, perishables, and some cold drinks for the drive. There was nothing worse about going on vacation, then having to go out food shopping after you got to your destination. So, when my parents rented a vacation home, we always brought our food to eliminate that chore.

To make vacation rentals more inconvenient, you couldn't get into your house until one or two in the afternoon. Owners needed time to clean and change linens. The icing on the cake was the hours renters spent in stop and go traffic, inching down the Garden State Parkway, to get to their destination. It's New Jersey's main thoroughfare to travel the length of the state, including shore points. In the summer, with the limited number of traffic lanes, it was a disaster, especially on weekends, as hundreds of thousands of cars headed to New Jersey beaches, including us, heading for LBI (Long Beach Island).

Even though my dad drove several hundred miles each week, selling industrial paints, he was tense about the drive, not knowing what the traffic situation would be like. That issue left his mind when he saw what I was carrying to the car.

180

"What in the world are you going to do with all that stuff?" he said, as I stood in front of him with my arms filled with radio equipment.

"I want to set up a radio station at Barnegat Light and send Morse code messages, just like the Coast Guard does to ships at sea," I said with excitement.

"Just be sure you don't knock out our TV reception down there. If you do, you'll be off the air in a flash and put on quiet hours," Dad warned.

That meant I could only transmit when Mom and Dad were not watching TV. There wasn't cable TV back in the fifties. Everyone used an antenna and got TV channel transmission signals from stations located in major cities, like NYC and Philadelphia. Sometimes reception was poor because of the distance from the station or from a bad antenna. On LBI, the TV antennas all pointed to Philadelphia, because it was closer than NYC.

"I'll be careful Dad; I can only send Morse code. You won't hear my voice squawking from the TV—that's a promise! I can't use voice until I get my General Class FCC License."

"Well, if there are black bars rolling up the TV screen, like railway tracks, every time you send a dot or dash, you're off the air." Dad pointed to an empty area and said, "Put those contraptions with your diving equipment, right here."

Dad closed the back hatch on the station wagon and a few minutes later, we were on our way. Back then, you had to drive some distance to get on the GS Parkway. This particular July day was beautiful but hot. The red line on the thermometer indicated 95F, but it was always cooler in Mendham because of all the shade trees. When we got to Union, the temperature must have spiked, probably nearing one-hundred degrees or more. Beads of sweat poured off our faces, as we used anything around us to fan ourselves. Like all other cars, ours was without air conditioning. Mom had packed several bottles of cola and sandwiches in the cooler. Since I sat in the back, I was the go-to person to distribute stuff, like snacks and soda.

We braced ourselves for the stalled traffic scene ahead. A long line of cars sat waiting to get on the toll highway. When I looked up at the Garden State Parkway Bridge, cars stood motionless like a car dealer's lot of unsold vehicles. This must have gone on for a while because several drivers had lifted their hoods to allow their engines to cool down. It was too late for one unfortunate family up ahead, as steam billowed and hissed from their car's radiator—just like Mom's steam iron when she pressed the black button!

Looking at Dad, he appeared to be disgusted; his attitude was heading south—I knew that from experience!

He slapped the steering wheel hard and shouted, "Damn! I knew this was going to happen!"

Sitting in the back seat, I added fuel to the fire when I said, "If you knew this was going to happen, why did you leave so late? I could've been skin diving in the ocean an hour ago!"

Dad turned his head and looked at me like he was ready to blow off steam too, just like the car on the side of the road ahead of us.

"I don't need advice from a back-seater, especially you!" he said.

I opened the cooler and passed out bottles of cola, it was my third, to cool everyone down, especially Dad.

About a half-hour later, the parkway traffic started moving and we got on our way. It took us about an hour to reach the Perth Amboy Bridge that goes over the Raritan River, when we came to a sudden stop, right at the very top of the bridge. After three bottles of cola, I needed to use a restroom or find a bunch of tall bushes. Stuck in traffic, one-hundred and thirty-three feet in the air, I knew neither of those options was available. What made the situation worse; I could see a humongous service and rest area on the other side of the bridge. I was racking my brain on what to do when a brilliant thought surfaced. *Jump out the car before Dad can say no and pee down off the bridge, and pray that a pleasure boat doesn't pass underneath at the same time.* The last thing I wanted to do was to tell my Dad I needed to go to the bathroom.

My brain was churning trying to come up with the gentlest of words to minimize his reaction to my plight. My mind was getting ready to mouth, *"Dad, you better get this car moving and moving fast,"* when divine intervention fell from the sky and traffic started moving, as I said, "Dad, I've got to go."

With the rest area packed, Dad had to park a distance away from the building. Almost before he got the car lever in park, I was out the back door running for the men's room. There were two cars exiting the lot, following close to one another blocking my way to the entrance door. I thought I had plenty of room when I zoomed by, in front of them. I heard the screech of brakes and knew I was wrong. Glancing back, I saw the skid marks on the pavement as the first guy came to an abrupt stop and the second car tapping the bumper of his vehicle. The guy closest to me stuck his head out the window and shouted, "Stupid jerk!" Then shoved his arm out the window, sticking out his middle finger to salute me. The second guy must have wanted to salute me too, as he did the same thing. That was a first for me!

Always respectful of the military, I saluted them back, the right way, with my right hand over my right eye. They looked surprised, like they were expecting me to salute them some other way.

After everyone did what they needed to do, we met back at the car with me getting a stern lecture.

"What were you thinking of? You nearly got run over!" Dad shouted.

"It was an emergency! What did you want me to do, pee all the way to the men's room?"

Five hours later, the weary and heat-drained vacationers picked up the rental house key at the realtor's office in Surf City.

Dad came out a few minutes later and we headed north to Barnegat Light.

He was in an awful mood about the drive, expressing that to Mom, and about the whole idea of coming to the Jersey shore for summer vacations.

"Jan, this is the last year we're doing this!"

When we got to the house, located on the ocean side of the island, close to the beach, I could smell the salty air. We unloaded the car. My body wanted to run to the beach, but my head told me to unpack the car, especially all the heavy items. I helped Dad finish unloading the car, as Mom put away the groceries and unpacked the cooler. I knew what was circling around in her head, as she was doing this, she expressed it each year. *"This is no vacation for me, having to make beds and cooking all the meals every day."*

Knowing supper would be sometime later, I headed for the ocean beach. As I got over the dunes, I could see it was high tide. I loved to walk near the water, dodging the waves, especially a rogue one that came occasionally. They could drench you or even pull you into the surf for the ride of your life. I kept my eye out for fishing lures and lead sinkers on my walk. I liked to collect them each summer. That effort was kind of useless though, since I didn't fish. I had gotten about a mile up the beach when I thought I should head back to the house for dinner. When I arrived back, I saw their plates half-eaten and knew I had arrived late. The aroma of Mom's Spanish rice with crumbled beef filled the house.

"Where were you? We waited and waited," Dad said in a grouchy tone.

"Beachcombing!"

Mom wasn't mad; she understood how much I liked the shore and placed a huge portion of food in front of me.

Later that evening, Mom and Dad were watching TV. Dad still looked exhausted from the drive with his eyelids drifting closed.

I had my hand on the doorknob, ready to go out the door with a roll of copper wire in my hand when his eyelids flashed open catching me in the act. But I beat him to the punch before he could say, "What are you going to do with that stuff?"

"I'm putting up an antenna in the dark, Dad, so no one will see me doing it—just like spies do!"

"Make sure you don't run that wire where I'll trip on it," he said with a worried look. He had that dreadful experience, nearly falling on his arse, a few times at home, in Mendham.

"Would a spy do something like that, Dad? Give away his location, so an FBI agent could just follow the wire and place him in handcuffs?" Dad just looked at me, with a serious face, over the top of his eyeglasses, not smiling a bit.

I made what radio enthusiasts call a random long wire antenna, one that's not tuned to any particular radio frequency. Using a small glass insulator, I tied one end to a pine tree that had seen better times, battered by countless nor'easters over the years. I snaked the other end through my bedroom window to an antenna tuner.

The transmitter that I built had two vacuum tubes, a 5U4G rectifier, and an 807 transmitting tube, all mounted to the top side of a steel box, called a chassis. I had to keep my fingers from the underside of the box because circuit voltages were up to seven hundred volts—enough to kill me!

While they watched TV, I organized my radio station, and then plugged-in my headset and telegraph key. I turned everything on, put on my earphones, and listened to various radio amateur stations sending code. I grabbed a pencil and jotted down some messages, wanting to join them, sending my dots and dashes.

The following morning, I got up early. All was quiet, they were still asleep, and most importantly, the TV was off. I turned on my equipment and tuned the antenna for the eighty-meter Novice ham band, using a crystal to transmit on a frequency of

3740 kHz. I started sending Morse code inviting other stations to converse with me.

After two hours of trying, I had no takers. Greatly disappointed, I flipped off the power switch and shut down my radio station. I looked at the clock and decided to visit my pals, Al and Sam. I changed into my bathing suit and matching T-shirt in case we wanted to go to the beach. I hoped luck would be with me, to get a glimpse of Kirsten. If that happened, that would be a good thing. But the bad part, if that happened, I'd be heartsick the rest of the day.

I walked up 4th street to their dark stained ranch house that sat on an elevated plot of land and spotted Kirsten sunning herself on the upper sun deck. I knocked on the door and my friends greeted me like a long lost pal. We shot the breeze on what to do that day and ended up doing nothing to avoid the heat and baking sun. When lunchtime approached, I said, "I'll see you guys tonight, at Andy's." That's where the lifeguards and teenagers gathered, along with Police Chief Flemming. He enjoyed rolling down his police car window to talk to us.

After dinner, before going to Andy's, I headed up the main drag to where the Coast Guard Station was located. The radio operator was listening to a Morse code message, maybe from a ship at sea, that blasted out of the observation windows. I admired the radioman's perfect sending and hoped that someday I could send as good as he could. After I listened for a while, I went on my way to our meeting spot.

****

We were lucky and had great weather during our vacation. I enjoyed being with my Mendham friends every day, especially hanging around with the lifeguards at night and shooting the breeze with Chief Flemming. I lucked out a few times, too, to see the most beautiful girl anywhere in the world—Kirsten. As far as my radio hobby, that was a washout. I was on the air for hours each day and didn't make one contact. Before I knew it, I was loading the car in the wee hours on Saturday morning so we would avoid traffic on our way home.

A week later, after we arrived back in Mendham, Dad came home from work, after stopping at the post office to pick up our mail. I was in my bedroom when he knocked on my door. I opened the door and he didn't look happy. He held a business envelope in his hand, waving it in front of me. I could see my name on it and Federal Communications Commission printed in red, on the right-hand upper corner.

"You're in big trouble!" Dad said, in a raised voice, out of breath, from racing to my room from his car. "You got the feds chasing after you now!" He slapped the FCC envelope in my hand.

With my heart racing, I put my finger under the seam and opened the envelope pulling the sheet out and unfolding it.

I read it, with Dad looking over my shoulder absorbing every word.

This is to inform you that your station, WV2NAV, was operating on a frequency of 7480 kHz from July 14th to the 27th, out of the amateur radio frequency band. Consequently, your signals interfered with a military teletype communications facility on Island Beach, New Jersey.

You are to cease and desist transmitting on this frequency immediately. Further interference will result in a fine of $500 per day the offense occurs and your radio license will be terminated. In addition, a warrant will be issued for federal marshals to seize your radio equipment.

I went back and read the FCC complaint again, looked at Dad and said, "I knocked out a military teletype? Can you believe that?"

"What in God's name were you doing broadcasting on a military channel? A $500 fine each day! Seizure of your equipment! Do you realize, they were probably blaming those damn Russians until they narrowed it down to you?

You better toss that transmitter in a garbage can right away, before the marshals grab it as evidence. Don't expect me to pay the fine!" Dad warned.

****

Back during the cold war, the Soviet Union purposely jammed Voice of America shortwave programs, so their citizens couldn't listen to them.

To do this, they had huge antennas and high-powered transmitters that sent a woodpecker sound across a wide band of short wave frequencies.

****

The teletype was the way information was sent worldwide by shortwave radio before the fax and internet. It was used by news organizations and the military for their primary communications. Unlike voice, it left a paper hard copy of what was sent and received.

****

"I know what happened, Dad. I had the transmitter tuned wrong. It transmitted on the second harmonic, sending my signal at twice my intended frequency, right on the military channel.

Next time Dad, I'll point my antenna at the Russians. Who knows, maybe I'll be on TV with the president pinning a medal on me and be known as something other than the mischievous kid from Mendham!"

Epilogue

I hope you enjoyed my journey as I reminisced about my childhood growing up in Mendham, NJ. For me, writing my mischievous stories wasn't only about the memory of them, but also about reliving them. Neuroscientists at MIT have discovered that memories are physical and can be reactivated; how true that was for me when I rolled back the calendar in my mind to begin writing my two books.

After writing my first book, *Mischievous in Mendham,* I had the opportunity to meet with one of my best childhood friends, Al, who is one of the main characters in both books. We had a wonderful time relating stories of the past. Sadly, Al's twin brother, Sam, had passed. I was also delighted to send a copy of my first book to Kirsten, their sister, whom I had secretly been in love with in my teens. She, of course, ended up being the story of Chapter 22, "Kirsten." With the help of social media, I was fortunate to have been able to get in contact with other classmates and folks that lived in Mendham during that time period. After publishing my book, I've received feedback from readers, strangers and friends alike, that has warmed my heart and brought a smile to my face.

Six decades later, I climb up on my bicycle, a Miyata 15-speed racing bike, to retrace my tour of Mendham that I had written about in the "Forward" section of this book. I start where Joe's Bar used to be, but it is long gone, replaced by a gas station. At a spry seventy-seven, I Pedal and balance, which proves to be a little more difficult than it was when I was 11, but I do alright, shifting down to make the long incline easier. Riding up the road, great stories emerge from my memory, some recorded in my books, others not. I take my time riding the bike about town as I attempt to relive that beautiful time in my life. Pascal Mercier, couldn't have said it better:

"We leave something of ourselves behind when we leave a place, we stay there, even though we go away. And there are things in us that we can find again only by going back there."

Pascal Mercier, *Night Train to Lisbon*

189

The author, age 14

Acknowledgments

I wish to thank Tom Cantillon, Instructor, Union College, for his brilliant suggestions along with those of the Chatham Creative Writers Group, all great writers; Dave, Ginny, Judy, Lillian, Matt, Max, Nabil, Parvis, and Sarah.

To the English major graduate, with the green pen, my sincere appreciation for all the extra help in making this book a great read—yeah, that's you, Sarah. I loved your neat notes along my page margins and all the haha's!

Barbara Henderson for making time in her busy schedule, to read, edit, and comment on each chapter—my gratitude and thanks.

My thanks and appreciation to, friend and fellow ham, Bob Willis for being my guide to climb up inside Hilltop Church's steeple. This journey helped jog my memory when I helped to install the two large speakers (metal horns) for the chime system years ago.

Also my thanks to my friend and classmate, Dick Willis, author and historian, who provided a wealth of information about Mountain Valley Pool and provided memorable photographs for this book.

To my lifelong friend, Dr. Alan Gibson, neuroscientist and computer whiz, who assisted me through both books with technical computer issues—my thanks to you, Alan.

Author's Notes

All the stories in this book were based on great memories of my childhood, growing up in Mendham Borough, New Jersey. For readers' enjoyment, the stories have been greatly embellished and creatively written by the author. This book should be considered a work of fiction for entertainment. Any resemblance to actual events and names, living or dead, are accidental. Aunt Holly was a character of my imagination.

Chapter 2, "Santa Claus and the Chimney," in *More Mischievous in Mendham* was the first story I wrote in narrative form and read out loud in a local library in a creative writing group, "Write Stuff," in Chester, NJ. There was so much laughter throughout my read that a librarian had to close our meeting room door because we were disrupting the other patrons.

At a later date, Tom Cantillon, an educator and long-time instructor of creative writers' groups suggested that I add dialog to this story. That brought the story to life, like you were right there with me, sitting on Santa Claus's lap holding his fake beard.

About the Author

Gregory Smith is a retired electronic technologist who worked in new product design, electronic test fixture design, and new product compliance to federal, military, and international standards for the Ohaus Corp. and ASCO Power Technologies/Emerson Network Power. Technical writing began at Gow-Mac Instrument Company writing instruction manuals for all their products. He attended both County College of Morris and National Radio Institute in Washington, D.C. Greg's interest in radio communication began in seventh grade when he became a radio amateur and then near retirement achieved his Advanced Class FCC License of W2GLS.

In 2006, he began writing for *Monitoring Times Magazine* with "Tales of a Teenage Radio Amateur," then became a regular writer for the magazine. Three of his stories were chosen as cover stories. "Who Really Invented Morse Code" unveiled the truth, that Alfred Vail was the real inventor of Morse code. "How to Catch a Spy," kept readers on the edge of their seats as the author and three other radio amateurs triangulated a spy's location in PA, reporting it to the FBI. Years later, CBS broadcasted on *"60 Minutes,"* "The Spy Among Us" believed to be the same spy.

In 2018 the author published his first book, *Mischievous in Mendham, a Collection of Childhood Memories*.

The writer is a member of Tom Cantillon's Creative Writers' Group in Chatham.